Essential Questions To Ask When Buying A House In France

and how to ask them

Mark Sampson

ACKNOWLEDGEMENTS

Of the many people who helped me with the raw material for this book, I would like to single out for particular thanks: Jessica Wall of *Celaur Immobilier* for all her time and meticulous attention to detail; Tim Mannakee for sharing his ideas and experience with such enthusiasm; Sophie Thompson for her customary generosity in helping me with the translations; Paul Foulkes for the technical information about all things electrical and for alerting me to the changes in TVA legislation; Steve Taylor for helping out on anything connected to plumbing and gas regulations; Waldemar Kaminski of *In Fin S* for providing insurance quotes; and Guy Williams for his interest, tales and insights.

Should you decide to go hunting for a house in France and your search takes you to the south-west, you can contact Jessica at celaurimmo@aol.com. Beaten down by his 'social charges', Paul Foulkes is no longer an electrician in France. He and his wife, however, have constructed a low-cost, low-energy house here and you can read about its construction and their ethos on their website, www.echohouse.eu. Tim Mannakee has given up building and renovation and is now a full-time photographer, who offers photography holidays in France. You can find out more on www.fleuretphotoholidays.com.

And thanks be to Dan Courtice, finally, for the front cover. A graphic artist by trade, you can contact him at dan@penngraphics.info.

Introduction

My wife, Deborah, and I have done it three times in roughly 15 years. Which is not excessive, but just often enough to reinforce the lessons of hindsight and to be able to speak with a certain degree of authority.

Ah, if we'd known then what we know now… The first time, it was a rush of blood to the head. We were in our thirties, which seemed awfully mature, but appears dangerously young now. I'd sold a share of a house in Brighton and we'd recently moved to Sheffield at a time when you could still buy a terrace-house as a Christmas present. We had money in our pockets and fancies in our head. For three weeks of a hot stormy summer at the end of the 1980s, we drove around the Dordogne and the Lot in a convertible Beetle to see what all the fuss was about. We took a tent, some clothes, a map and some sales literature from the few UK agents that specialised at that time in French properties. If the Internet existed, I wouldn't have known how to use it.

By the end of our holiday, we had signed a contract for a stone farmhouse in the Corrèze. It proved far too big for us and not quite as habitable as we had surmised. The village it abutted proved to be a hotbed of internecine jealousies and family squabbles. The climate was not as hot and sunny as it had seemed during our scouting trip. But it cost our requisite £15,000. We took out a loan with the Alliance & Leicester to pay the legal fees, and the place – more by chance than by foresight – would prove an adequate and generally happy family home for the first eight years of our self-imposed exile. However… had we borrowed a little more money and asked some of the essential questions that we didn't know enough to ask, we might have bought something in an up-and-coming picturesque town like Martel and watched a shrewd investment appreciate before our very eyes. But that's the wonder of hindsight.

The second time, it was a matter of necessity. One of the questions we failed to ask when we bought the farmhouse concerned the arrangements *vis à vis* the little attached house next door. Of course it was sheer lunacy to buy a house that had been divided into two by bickering brothers. The smaller annexe next door was rented by the old couple across the road to an ex-soldier who smoked limp roll-ups and recounted his experiences in Algeria and Vietnam. He lived, we discovered later, in abject squalor. When he moved out, the proprietors installed a surly man who would sweep into our shared courtyard at the end of his working day and often proceed to take a leak against the garage door. The folly of our purchase really hit home. Having lived happily in a row of Victorian terrace houses, the prospect of attached neighbours hadn't seemed such a big deal. These ones proved as invasive as chronic indigestion. Somehow, we'd completely missed the whole point of buying a house in the French countryside: which is surely to get away from it all and live in the kind of splendid detachment that money rarely buys in the UK. We realised that we would never find anyone as daft as us to buy it in its current situation. So when the infirm proprietors proposed to offload it to their English neighbours (who surely had more money than sense), we jumped at the chance of sole ownership. £25,000 seemed quite a lot for what amounted to a two-up two-down, but it meant that we could undo the damage done by the warring siblings and use the annexe as a (singularly unsuccessful) *gîte*.

By the third time of doing it, I had passed 50 and we were veterans of a decade in a foreign land. The reality of approaching retirement with little provision made for our 'third age' prompted executive action. We bought a solid semi-detached stone house in Brive with a loan from La Poste. It would serve as a treatment centre for Deborah's aromatherapy practice, with an apartment above big enough for a small family. The anticipated income would just about meet the monthly repayments. By now we were wise enough to ask the right questions.

This is a book, then, to guide you through the process of buying your own place in France – if that's what you decide that you *really* want to do – by steering you clear of some of the pitfalls into which we (and certain other friends and acquaintances) have unwittingly stepped. By common consent, these are the essential questions that you need to ask – not just of significant others, but also of yourself. Do you, for example, want to buy a house to live in either full-time or part-time or simply as an investment? If, say, it's for living in *définitivement*, are you quite sure that you know what's involved? I know plenty of people who have done it and made a go of it – and have asked them for contributions, born of their successful experience, to the list of essential questions. Equally, I know those who haven't made it and, for some reason or other, have decided to sell up and go back home – often because of a failure to examine the fundamental reality of buying property in a foreign country.

Among my acquaintances, a couple in their 30s have bought an old hotel. It wasn't very expensive and, having sold their property in the UK, they can't be short of a few euros. It's situated at the side of an old *Route Nationale*, but all the passing traffic now uses the adjacent motorway. It will cost at least what they paid for the building itself to bring it up to a standard that will suit today's potential clientele. Neither of them speaks any French, so they're hoping to attract English-speaking guests (even though it's located in an area that tends to be by-passed in the race to the sunny south). I wish them all the luck in the world, but I can't help but wonder what on earth they are thinking of.

Forgive me if at times I sound a tad cynical or paint a gloomy picture. If, having read this book, you can place your hand on your heart and say, 'Yes thanks, I'm clear in my mind that I want to do this – and I know how to go about it', then it has served its purpose.

I should say at this point that this book is *not* designed to serve as a comprehensive handbook. While I try wherever possible and appropriate to provide some helpful up-to-date information, bear in mind that regulations (especially those that emanate from our dearly beloved European Commission) change with alarming regularity. So don't take this 'as gospel'. I see this more as a useful framework to guide you logically through the whole process, to be supplemented (if you want to learn more) by at least one of the very good publications already on the market.

You'll find the questions divided into a number of sections that correspond roughly with the various stages of the process you will find yourself going through. Although the answers I provide are as detailed as I feel it helpful at this stage, you may nevertheless want to ask certain questions of someone like an estate agent for any further useful views and ideas. Questions that you may have to ask of French people – in different shapes and guises – have been translated in the summary at the end of each chapter (with a pronunciation guide that will, hopefully, obviate those awful stultifying looks of blank incomprehension). You may, of course, discover other questions (relevant to your own particular circumstances) that you should ask along the way, but these are the basic ones germane to most purchases.

Chapter 1. *Why do I want to buy a house in France?*

Recent refugees from the UK paint a gloomy picture of life in the mother country. Can it really be as bad as all that? Is it going relentlessly down the pan? I certainly hope not. I wonder sometimes whether we don't allow ourselves to get swept out to sea with our brethren on a raft of the media's making. So this chapter poses some basic questions to encourage you to explore your motivation. We're very happy here, but it's not all a bowl of cherries across the Channel. French life creates its own unique set of problems. If the idea of acquiring French property (either to live in or to invest in) is partly induced by malaise, are you sure that you're not romanticising the whole house-in-France notion?

I hope by the time you reach the end of this chapter that you'll be quite sure that you really want to do this. Or not, as the case may be.

Q 'Why France?'

I have a couple of friends nearby who are organic farmers. He's Dutch and she's English. When they decided they wanted to be organic farmers, they also decided that they wanted to live and farm somewhere other than Britain or the Netherlands. They looked around in Portugal and in Spain (the real Spain and not the pretend Spain of the *costas*). One day while watching a wrinkled sun-scorched peasant farmer herding his goats, they recognised that such people would be their only neighbours. The woman pictured herself popping into a bar – and a host of male eyes fixing her askance. It was all just too different. So then they looked in France. The countryside was green, the climate was mild, the property was (then) inexpensive and it was that much closer to their respective homes. The language and culture were different, but it still felt more familiar. They bought a farm irrigated by the Dordogne in summer, and they have stayed there happily ever since.

So why do so many of us Brits gravitate towards a country that has inspired and continues to inspire quite ambivalent feelings? France is a foreign country, but the Channel is narrow enough to swim. The people are different, but we have loved them as familiar enemies for hundreds of years: they conquered us and then we conquered some of them and then, because we helped them out of a pickle in the second world war, they feel grateful and resentful at the same time and love-hate us more than ever. They might speak a different language, but it's one we generally try to learn (rather unsuccessfully) at school. The culture is unfamiliar, but not so unfamiliar as it is in Greece or Bulgaria. Administration and customer service are dreadful, but it's probably worse in Italy. Property is plentiful and cheaper than it is in the UK, but it's not as cheap as it is in Romania or Croatia. The food and wine are good, but not as good as they're cracked up to be. The climate's rather better than our own, but not as extreme as it is in Spain or Portugal. The cost of living may be slightly higher, but the quality of life is better. And, of course, it's eminently accessible by road, rail and air.

So why *not* buy property in France?

Q 'What's my motive for buying a house in France?'

If you simply want to dabble in French property, you could buy a house or a flat as an investment and rent it out to others until you are ready to sell. If you like the lifestyle sufficiently, you could buy somewhere as a holiday house. Or you could go the whole hog and move to France.

Q 'Should I buy a house as an investment?'

It's certainly not a bad idea. Much depends on the area that you choose, because property in some parts of the country tends to appreciate faster than it does in others. Generally – and based on trends over the last few years when prices have risen consistently after a fairly long period of stagnation – property prices are more stable than they are in the UK. Steady growth (in recent years, before The Great Recession, at around an annual 10 per cent mark) rather than cycles of boom and bust seems to be the hallmark. FNAM (The Fédération Nationale de l'Immobilier) – one of the two professional bodies to which most French estate agents will belong – publishes a monthly analysis of the property market on its website (www.fnaim.fr). After ten consecutive years of rising prices between 1998 and 2007, two years of falling prices followed. 2010 then saw an average rise of 2 per cent, while prices rose by 7.3 per cent in 2011 – but it would be a brave individual who would forecast a further rise in 2012.

French *agents immobiliers* (estate agents), of course, are as guilty as their UK colleagues of 'talking up' the market. It's hardly surprising, I suppose, given that their fees for a sale are around 8 per cent, which is an awful lot when you consider that that the 'top whack' for a UK agent is something like 2.5 per cent. Given the level of the various agents' and legal fees associated with buying and selling property in France, along with a general feeling that the real breathtaking bargains are now a thing of the past, it would certainly make an investor looking for a big and/or speedy return think twice about buying a house here.

Nevertheless, there is an interesting scheme sponsored by the French government. French leaseback property is, they say, 'one of the best kept secrets of the property investing world'. Although established many years ago now, it's certainly not common knowledge that this scheme allows investors in qualified leaseback developments to claim back the 20 per cent TVA (the French equivalent of VAT) they pay on the price of the property. In return, the government reaps the reward of having tourists with money to spend stay in the property that you own. Although you own the property outright, you agree to hand it over for a fixed term (from 9 to 11 years maximum) to a management company that in return guarantees to pay you a net return of something like 4.5–6 per cent of the cost of the property. So if you buy a house for, say, €120,000, you would actually only pay around €100,000 because the TVA element of the sale is re-funded. If the guaranteed return were 6 per cent, you would receive an annual income of roughly €6,000. At the end of the period, the management company returns the property to you – to deal with as you wish. What's more, leasebacks appear to be exempt from attempts to levy French tax on second homes for non-residents. This is somewhat simplified and there are a few caveats (the risk, for example, that the developers go bust and thus scupper the 'letting' agreement), but if you want to know more then you can download a free guide at www.jamesgreenandco.co.uk (just one of several property consultants that can steer you in this direction), or contact them by telephoning 01624 828701.

Leaseback aside, you can place your investment property in the hands of a good agent and let him or her do the hard work in return for a not unreasonable fee. However, French law favours the tenant over the landlord and if you get saddled with a rogue incumbent, you could find yourself embroiled in some Dickensian legal action. We'll look at some of the legal issues of renting – be it short- or long-term – in Chapter 8.

When it comes to selling the property, there are certain legal and fiscal pitfalls to consider. TVA and capital gains legislation is fairly complicated (isn't it always?), and you might find yourself with large bills to pay that take big chunks out of the return on your investment. Again, we'll look at these issues in Chapter 8.

Q 'Should I buy a house in France as a holiday home?'

Since France is still the most popular holiday destination for Brits (indeed, the most visited country in the world, with over 77 million visitors annually), you would be in good company. Given the country's popularity, you could probably find a fair number of friends and relatives who will want to use the house when you're not there and who might well be prepared to contribute to its upkeep.

But… having bought our first French house for this purpose, I sometimes question the wisdom of the holiday-home option. For one thing, you tie yourself down to a particular location year in and year out. Moreover, to get the most out of your house, you'll probably want to come out at least two or three times per year – which can all get rather expensive. The more you visit, the more (hopefully) you'll love your retreat – but the more emotional 'dissonance' you might experience. The good thing about a conventional holiday is that you know it's a finite thing: at the end of a week or two, it's over and you can return home with some happy memories and some nice snaps to show people and get back to real life. Whereas we found that every time we left our holiday home in the Corrèze and embarked on the long haul back to Sheffield, the wrench of leaving got more and more difficult to endure – with the result that we became increasingly dissatisfied with real life and couldn't wait to get back to our other home. You start thinking that a holiday could be for life and not just two or three weeks of every year.

If your new holiday home requires some degree of renovation, there's a real danger that you could be wearing yourself out rather than recuperating from the daily grind. Even if you decide not to do the work yourself, there will be materials to source and workers to mobilise.

On top of this, there is the expense to consider of keeping your holiday home legal and insured and in the style to which you have become accustomed. There are plenty of kind neighbours around who will volunteer to keep a watchful eye on your property and open the shutters the day before your arrival and such like. Nevertheless, there are storms and heavy rain and roof tiles slip and you find yourself wondering what's happening hundreds of miles away from your principal residence. And if there's work to organise, it's hard enough to do it when you're *in situ*, let alone back in the UK.

So a French holiday home can be lovely, but you want to be quite sure that you appreciate just what the trade-off could be for those precious two or three weeks of tranquil evening meals on the terrace.

Q 'Should I buy a house in France to live in?'

We come to the third option. There are something like 250,000 British nationals already living either full-time or part-time in France. What's more, as increasing numbers of younger people find themselves priced out of the UK property market, almost a third of first-time buyers are now opting to buy abroad as an alternative. Many of them will choose France. So are you one of the several thousand annually who want to move to France lock, stock and barrel?

If you are, then you want to make absolutely sure that the house you decide to buy is the right house in the right area, because the upheaval of moving across the Channel is not one that you would wish to repeat too soon. And you want to be fairly sure that you can make a real go of it. Such is the gulf in property prices that it would be too hard to swap a spacious family home here for a cramped terrace house in somewhere like Preston.

Personally, I agonised over this for aeons, drawing up lists of pros and cons on flipchart paper, driving myself and my wife so crazy in the process that finally we said, 'Oh come on, let's just do it', which is maybe not the soundest basis for such a momentous decision. This is such a big question to consider that we should divide it up into a number of more manageable sub-questions.

'How easy will it be to support ourselves in France?'

The answer boils down to some kind of Micawber-like equation: whether your anticipated incomings can accommodate your regular outgoings. You hear conflicting things about the cost of living. Officially, the UK is a more expensive place to live in than France. My impression, as part of a self-employed family, is that the cost of living averages out rather higher here. If alcohol is cheaper in France, food, clothes, furniture, building materials, white goods, cars all cost more. The cost of running your car is a little cheaper and insurance is on a par with UK premiums. The combined property taxes probably add up to less than most council tax assessments. Running a telephone and a television costs more or less the same. There's not much in it when it comes to income tax, but there are all kinds of stealth taxes that make the French fiscal burden one of the heaviest in Europe. Certainly, if you're self-employed and you have to pay the equivalent of National Insurance contributions, you will be flabbergasted by the quarterly bills. Nor, of course, is health care free, so you will need to factor in the cost of either full or top-up insurance. Even eating out is not quite the bargain that we often suppose. So make sure that, as the Americans say, you 'do the math'.

If you are employed or retired – with a pension – you will probably manage. Particularly as shopping is not quite the social obsession that it is in the UK. Apart from the pre-Christmas panic, shops are still mainly shut on Sunday. The fabled French quality of life is more about enjoying the kinds of natural pursuits that generally come free.

If you are self-employed, you could find it more of a struggle. Self-employment is seen by the French government not as an opportunity to create national wealth and employment, but a chance to extract taxes, direct and indirect. So should you need to employ anyone from a gardener to a roofer, you will find yourself paying more than you would in the UK.

Most ex-pats manage to get by, but it's not easy and you will probably never get rich. Be aware that – without some kind of regular income – you may have to temper your ambitions and 'hustle to survive', and mentally you'll be better prepared for the venture.

'What are my prospects for finding work here?'

In all honesty – unless you're prepared to create your own opportunities for gainful employment – they're not very good. French society does not embrace competition. People and enterprises tend to sniff at the idea. Protectionism, despite the decrees of the European parliament, is still rife. Though there seems to be an insatiable demand for holiday accommodation (which you could manage or service), disavow yourself of any notion of, say, driving a little yellow van and delivering the post.

Professionals with hard-earned supposedly international qualifications will, as likely as not, find that these have no more value than the paper they're printed on. Despite official bleating about the nation's inability to speak English, for example, it is still decreed that French children should be taught to 'spick ze Eengleesh' by French-born teachers who have acquired their linguistic skills via the academic route. I have an old college friend who married a Frenchman around 30 years ago. She has lived in the Alps ever since and is, to all intents and purposes, a bilingual French native now. Theoretically highly qualified, after years of trying she finally managed to obtain a position as an English *assistante* in a French school. She was given an annual contract, which she managed to renew twice, and was paid peanuts. Now, as if to underline the lack of value accorded to English-speaking *assistants*, her post has been given to a visiting student from New Zealand.

Realistically – unless you are employed out here by a company with UK links – your best bet is self-employment. My wife Deborah receives constant e-mails and calls from UK aromatherapists interested in setting up over here. She has to tell them that because of a rigid medical framework, the profession is not officially recognised here and she herself has to operate in a quasi-legal capacity. In these rural parts, most ex-pats either run *gîtes* for the holiday market or make some kind of a living as carpenters, plumbers, electricians, plasterers, estate agents, private English tutors or caretakers of holiday homes. Many open up bedrooms in their lovingly restored homes as *chambres d'hôte*, but – when you think that there is even a book dedicated to the subject of running *chambres d'hôte* in *south west* France – you have to ask just how many this niche market will tolerate. There seem to be plenty of writers and artists over here, but few – apart from our friendly neighbourhood American best-selling novelist – make much of a living and most have to rely on other forms of financial support. I suppose you could always find yourself a very recherché niche in the market like a friend (with a Metropolitan Police pension) who set himself up in Brittany for a (limited) time as a grower and installer of willow hedges.

Finding work is no doubt easier near or in big cities, but few *immigrés* want to buy a house in a town, let alone a city. Self-employment sometimes seems to be the only option, but it isn't easy and you should research the local market well to make sure that it can bear the strain of another piano teacher, for instance. Bear in mind that 25 per cent of the work force here is employed by the state. The *fonctionnaire*, the not very *civil* servant, is still god; the self-employed entrepreneur is someone merely to stoke the hungry maw of *l'administration*. Whatever optimistic politicians claim, the French economy is stagnant, even moribund. Ordinary people seemed, at least until the *crise*, to look upon the UK as a kind of Land of Opportunity (without wishing to countenance the kinds of reforms necessary to create more employment opportunities). As a job seeker from the UK, you can register for work at the local branch of the A.N.P.E. (*Agence Nationale pour l'Emploi*), the French equivalent of the job centre. If you have been receiving Job Seeker's Allowance in the UK for at least the previous four weeks, in theory you keep your right to receive it at the current UK rate. In practice, it takes so long that you will probably have starved to death or given up and gone back to the UK by the time you see the first cheque. In order to try it, bring with you an E303 and UBL22 and present them when you register at the ANPE (within seven days of arriving here). *Bon courage*. Although French TV a few years ago broadcast a programme exposing the number of Brits signing on for and creaming off state benefits, I haven't yet encountered a single individual who has received a single *cent d'euro* via French social security.

So… self-employment (*profession libérale*) it usually has to be. Given the French capacity for bureaucratic complexity, it isn't as difficult as it might seem to register as such. When you go along to an office of URSSAF or the *Chambre de Métiers* in your departmental (sub-) prefecture (the equivalent of 'county town'), you will usually find them only too pleased to advise you how to do it – and how to pay your swingeing charges. Until the advent of the *auto-entrepreneur*, most people opted initially for the *micro-enterprise* route. If you are offering a service, you can opt for this route provided that you earn (currently) under €32,000 per annum. If you are re-selling goods and materials, your annual turnover must be less than €80,000. Roughly three quarters of your gross income is treated as allowable expenses and you are taxed on the remaining fraction. Your annual tax declaration is much easier, so there is no need to use the services of a *comptable* (accountant). Although it works very well if your income remains roughly under the €20,000 mark, once it goes over this level you can end up actually paying more tax than if you are registered under the *réel* (standard) regime. With its application of tax credits and deduction of allowable expenses, the standard regime will be more familiar to anyone who has been self-employed in the UK. In most circumstances, once your turnover exceeds €32,000 per annum (or €80,000 if you are re-selling goods and materials), you become liable to pay and claim back TVA. Accountants here can charge the earth for their services because the various fiscal declarations are so complicated and time-consuming.

The *auto-entrepreneur* scheme was one of the few genuinely radical (for France) acts of the Sarkozy government. It has made it much easier to launch a more speculative service or business, because your tax and social contributions together are levied monthly at a fixed rate (currently 23% of your income, if you provide a service) based on your actual earnings for the previous month. In other words, you don't pay anything if you didn't earn anything in a particular month. Although this might sound standard and logical, it is a disarmingly simple concept for

France. So simple, in fact, that it has created all kinds of resentment among those who do it the hard way. Typically, The Powers have told artisans that they will make their lives easier not be relieving them of some of their fiscal and administrative burden, but by making things harder for *auto-entrepreneurs*. 'Hang down your head and cry...'

'If you are in a relationship, is your partner really committed to this dream?'

This is such a fundamental question that I should maybe have inserted it as the first issue to address if you're considering buying a house to live in permanently. Since, however, many of the problems among couples arise when one partner finds work and the other stays at home, this could be the most appropriate point.

Where I've heard of things going badly wrong, it's often to do with a relationship suffering as a result of the abnormal strains placed upon it by a fairly unique set of circumstances. What can happen is that Partner A has a very strong dream. So strong that Partner B is swept along in its current. It's easier sometimes just to go along with it. Besides, maybe Partner B *should* go along with it: try something new and adventurous rather than always opting for what seems safe and secure. So Partner B acquiesces and they move out here and there's a honeymoon period when everything seems rather wonderful and exciting. But then Partner A goes out to work and makes friends and has a good old sociable time with them, but Partner B's left at home, holding the fort (and perhaps the baby at the same time). Soon, the whole experience seems to pall. Despite his or her best efforts, Partner B finds it hard to make some new friends and misses all the friends left behind. Loneliness creeps in. There's tension between them because Partner A seems to be happy and positive, whereas Partner B feels like a wet blanket. Tension simmers and sporadically erupts. And... well, you know what happens.

I heard, for example, a rather sad tale of a Dutch couple that moved to the region to open a restaurant. It's a lovely house in a gorgeous village. He was very committed to the idea and worked hard to make it a success. It became increasingly clear, however, that her heart wasn't in the venture to quite the same degree. Whereas he enjoyed all the sociable aspects of catering – chatting with the customers, earning the plaudits, generally being the host with the most – she discovered that it wasn't as she had imagined it: the hours were long, the work was laborious, there was little down-time and the language was hard to master. Because she was lonely and missed everyone back home in the Netherlands, she eventually told him that she wasn't happy and couldn't stay here any longer. She moved back to the old country, while he stayed on to keep the restaurant open and frequented. For a while, they managed to keep both things going: restaurant and relationship. But long-distance love proved too impractical. The restaurant is still open and he's happy at its helm, but the relationship fizzled out.

So if you're planning to do this as a couple, be as sure as you possibly can that it's not just one person's dream. Be realistic about what might be involved. Anticipate how it might feel if you're going to be on your own for any length of time without work in strange new surroundings – and plan accordingly. You could, for example, sign up for an informal conversation group as a means of learning or improving your French. Or pursue hobbies and interests via some of the many private associations that could offer an opportunity to meet other people while honing your language skills. Once you feel a little more confident and rather less self-conscious about communicating with local people, you can often find ways of taking a sufficiently active part in the life of your chosen community.

'How will we manage without our family and friends?'

I suppose the answer to this question depends on how (dys)functional your family is. A move abroad can represent an ideal opportunity to get away from all the guilt and the hang-ups, or at least it offers a ready excuse and an invaluable breathing space.

On the other hand... the difficulty of being in a strange land without that familiar safety net can be intensified by living and working with people for whom the family plays such an important role. The French aren't quite Italians or Spanish in that respect, but they are a close-knit bunch all the same. In my experience, French children don't tend to stray too far when it's time to leave the nest, so families often live within hailing distance of each other: to eat together on a Sunday, to help out with DIY projects and to do all the things that a family is supposed to do. We kidded ourselves that we didn't need all that, while secretly looking on with a certain yearning for such closeness and security. Especially when our daughter was very young. Very often here, where the parents both go out to work, the grandparents will play a more prominent role as surrogate parents (rather than a mere distraction) to the children, readily administering the *fessées* that they administered to their own children in an era when smacking was more the norm. The state also encourages the concept of the extended family by offering generous financial help to parents prepared to go that little bit further for the motherland – by spawning three or more children.

In practice, this means that the family unit usually has everyone and everything it needs on its doorstep; why should it admit those (admittedly charming and rather amusing) foreigners from down the road busily trying to cultivate new friendships? On arriving here with a 10-month old baby, it was a shock to discover that locals were really not that interested in our suggestions for communal playgroups and mutual baby-sitting. It was a hard lesson: that they didn't need us as much as we needed them.

So... either, as some canny people seem to do, you import sundry members of your family, find them a nice house nearby and carry on as before, or you build up a network of friends to serve as some kind of ersatz extended family. It's always hard to move away from friends, but – whether you move from Southend to Swansea or Siddcup to Saint-Étienne – you usually end up making new ones easily enough. Besides, we reasoned, how often do you see your closest friends? Even those who lived nearby we probably saw once a month at most. They could come and see us in France and we would see each other for a whole week at a time, which probably added up to a longer period than all those soirées and cinema trips combined. We could spend real quality time with our old friends. But visitors all usually want to come in the summer when the weather is fine and even a week can be a long time if someone keeps throttling your toothpaste tube, or doesn't like brown rice, or isn't willing to help with the washing-up because they're on holiday. If you're not careful, you can spend the entire summer catering and fetching and carrying. It's both disruptive and exhausting.

The more practical species of friend is someone on the end of a telephone, who can pop round and share a cup of something hot and exchange moans or look after the children when you have to nip down to the prefecture to see about changing your driving license. Would we ever manage to find friends like that in a foreign country? I suppose the temptation is to panic somewhat – like a diffident swimmer who suddenly realises that his or her feet can no longer touch the bottom – rather than to relax and let the water buoy you up. If anything, and provided you're aware that a shared language is not necessarily the firmest basis for friendship, it can be easier to make new friends among an English-speaking community abroad than back in the UK. Everyone's in the same boat and often only too willing to help. It's like network marketing. You get invited to one 'do' and you meet couple B, who know person C, who's a good friend of person D, who's also a market gardener with a similar passion for philately, and before you know it you have more friends than you can shake a stick at. Indeed, there comes a time when you reach saturation point, whereupon you can sit back and take stock and sort out the genuine friends from the casual acquaintances.

In short, unless you're exceptionally self-contained and/or deeply misanthropic, you won't manage well without family and friends. On the other hand, you can manage quite nicely if you make enough new friends for an active social life.

'How easy will it be to adapt from city to rural life?'

This may seem like an innocuous question to ask yourself. Don't, however, neglect to ask it. In many ways, herein lies the rub. The radical change lies just as much in the move from one lifestyle to another as it does in swapping one country for another. Most people who move to France – I believe – are town or city dwellers wanting a part of the *in*action, i.e. less of the hurly burly and more of the peace and quiet and space and countryside for which France is renowned. It's a question that's just as relevant to someone thinking of swapping a flat in Chelsea for a Cumbrian cottage on the outskirts of Kirby Stephen. It sounds great for a periodic retreat, but the whole year round? If cinema, theatre, concerts, restaurants and/or major sporting events (as opposed to pig-racing in the main street of your nearest market town) are essential to your happiness, you should plump for somewhere that's a short drive from somewhere like Lyon or Toulouse.

Tourism is essential to this country's wealth and happiness and if you choose an area that has its fair share of visitors, there's often a load of interesting things going on. But only for two or three months each summer. As a music fanatic, I'm staggered by the sheer wealth of festivals, big and small, during July and August. However, there are only so many you can attend in the same month (or sometimes the same weekend!). Come October and even the most bustling of small towns will go into hibernation. Knowing that, we moved to France (in the days before play.com) with boxes and boxes of books and videotapes, equipped to drip-feed our own culture throughout the long winter months. They kept us going till the advent of Freeview and DVD boxed sets.

Obviously the rhythms and 'mind-set' of rural life are totally different to those of the city. The positive side of it is that you become (unless you buy your property on, say, the Côte d'Azur) much more aware of the changing seasons. People revert to the basic animal at the core of their being: cutting wood and gathering fruit and vegetables to freeze, bottle, pickle and jam at the end of the summer; doing all those outstanding maintenance jobs during the mild days of autumn in order to make the nest as cosy and weatherproof as possible; closing the shutters and huddling by the wood-burning fire during the dark days of winter; emerging to fill the lungs and plant and think once more about all those things that animals do in the spring time; taking it all a little easier and enjoying the company of fellow humans once again during the protracted days of summer.

Sounds idyllic really. And it can be. On the negative side, however, small-community mentality (be it French, ex-pat or both) can drive you gravely insane. Unless you go for somewhere so far off the beaten track that no one knows you're there, everyone will know or want to know your business. It's not so bad in our current location, but when we lived at the edge of a small village, every time you set foot outdoors you could feel hidden pairs of eyes furtively regarding your every move. I couldn't even bang a nail in without someone coming by to check whether I'd banged it in correctly or crookedly. In a big city, you can preserve a certain healthy anonymity. In a small rural community, your private life is bigger news than the presidential elections.

Beatrix Potter wrote a charming book called *The Tale of Johnny Town Mouse*. Read and think on't!

'What will it be like in winter?'

Not particularly easy. Perhaps one of the reasons for France's popularity has something to do with a touching notion that the weather is always good here. Briançon in the French Alps (the highest town in Europe) might boast 300 days of sunshine per year, and maybe they do indeed have warm wet winters with westerly winds on the Med, but really things aren't *that* different from the UK here weather-wise. There's a good chance that if it's fine in the UK, it'll be fine in France – and vice versa. Choose to settle in Normandy or Brittany or somewhere along the Atlantic coast, and you can expect a temperate climate subject to the prevailing winds similar to the south of England. However, once you move towards the centre of the country, it becomes more continental. Which means that, yes, summers are longer and warmer than they are back home, but winters can be surprisingly harsh. The good thing is that they are rarely grey and neutral ('neither mickling, nor muckling' as Billy Liar teased Councillor Duxbury); they are real winters – with plenty of those bracing sunny days when the leafless trees take on the appearance of cardboard cut-outs. Snow can fall. Up in the mountains, said snow can hang around from November till April – but then the community is geared up for it.

No, it's not necessarily the weather you should beware of in winter. It's the hard work involved in keeping warm should you opt for some romantic draughty stone house heated exclusively by wood-burning fires. And, above all, it's the fact that everything and everyone tends to wind down operations for the duration.

I once drove up into the *Haute* Corrèze to interview a young woman in connection with an article about the late-lamented Trans-Corrézian railway line. Her office was high up in the building shared by the *mairie* and the *école primaire*. It's a lovely area and the town itself is pretty enough. But that day it was grey and wet and, apart from the sound of children in the playground and a few passing cars, there was no sign of life. A ghost town. Even the little *boulangerie* was shut for the afternoon. She told me about an English couple who had bought a house there. One winter was all it took to drive them back to Blighty.

Even in the rain, there's something charming about a maritime community off-season. In the heart of the country, however, where accordion music and obscure card games represent traditional entertainment, you run the risk of going stir crazy in winter.

'Are we likely to be accepted as part of the community?'

It's very difficult to say. Let's start with a salutary lesson told me by a friend. A carpenter and his wife had seen a nice old stone farmhouse in mid-summer and had fallen in love with it. When they moved out to their new home in the Back of Beyond, however, they found that the house was daubed with obscene slogans. The hamlet, it transpired, was owned by various progenitors and offspring of a singularly unpleasant farmer. He and his clan set out to make life as unpleasant as possible for the new arrivals. Whenever they wanted to go into town for some shopping or building materials, they would find tractors and machinery blocking their exits. No one spoke to them; shoulders were as cold as the winter. Nevertheless, the carpenter tried to win over the natives by building the head a wooden table for the family kitchen. When they took it along to a party at The Big Farm, honcho and henchman manhandled it out into the courtyard, told them that the peace offering was not wanted and showed them the door. Eventually and unsurprisingly, the carpenter's wife threw in the towel and went back to the UK. The carpenter stayed on to finish the refurbishment work he had started. But when it came to trying to sell the house, the farmer made it clear to every prospective buyer that they weren't wanted there. Finally, the carpenter sold the house to the head honcho for the price he had originally paid, writing off in the process his time, effort, money and angst.

A clever pre-meditated con-trick or shades of *Straw Dogs*? One of the points of this cautionary tale is that such a thing doesn't happen very often and, if it does, it could equally happen in deepest Cornwall as it could in *France profonde*. Another point is that you have to try to gauge the community within which you are intending to settle. People are always suspicious of newcomers and few relish change. If, however, you suspect that no one for miles around has ever ventured outside the *département*, they may just be suspicious to the point of paranoia. It's not necessarily anything personal or even anything to do with your nationality. It's a well-known fact that the French hate the English as much as we hate them. On the other hand, they love and admire us (begrudgingly) as much as we (reluctantly) love and respect them. When they go to a British party, they love the way we let our hair down and dance (as Betjeman might have it) 'until it's *tea* o'clock'. When we go to a French party, we love the food and the wine and, because everything is done so elegantly, we are happy to wait until it has all been properly digested before pushing the chairs back and letting go (till it's time for the onion soup to materialise in the wee small hours). The relationship is a notoriously complicated one.

When we moved over in 1995, we had this idealistic notion that we didn't want to live anywhere near Brits on the grounds that we had come to live in France and not in Little Britain. So we did our level best to integrate and, to a degree, we were accepted by the community. We were always known as *les Anglais*, but then the Parisian holidaymaker was always known as *le Parisien*. Although we stuck out like sore thumbs, our fellow *communards* were intrigued by (if ultimately dismissive of) our different set of beliefs and ways of doing things. Funnily enough, it was the older people of the village who took to us more readily than some of the younger arrivals. Maybe it was a jealousy thing: being a writer, I was never spied earning the money that must have appeared to grow on our trees, whereas I apparently had enough time on my hands to walk the infant and, a few years later, the dog; or hack ineffectually at our recalcitrant garden; or attempt – regrettably – to Do It Myself. Sensing, perhaps, that we must have felt isolated and a little lonely, people would tell us with great excitement that they had a friend in a village seven kilometres distant who knew a retired Scottish teacher who came to these parts during the summer months. Apart from inviting a retiring Welsh oceanographer to dinner one evening, we generally resisted the temptation to investigate such sightings.

The degree to which, after 12 years of owning the house, we were accepted by the community can be gauged by the party that a group of French friends threw for us. It took place on the evening before we moved to the plot of land on which we would build our current home. Everyone gave us a present and it was a very touching affair and I felt genuinely sad at the thought of leaving. At one point in the evening, however, I remember looking around and thinking: how many of these people do I really know anything about? At most there are maybe three couples we still consider good friends. Yet, after only a few years in an area where there are many more ex-pats per hectare, we have more friends and a busier social life than we ever did in either Sheffield or Brighton.

C'est comme ça, as they say. The fact is we're different. While our mother tongues and our cultures share certain recognisable origins, they are as different now as cheddar and Camembert. The French sense of humour assimilates only Benny Hill, Mr. Bean and the more puerile aspects of Monty Python. Individually and collectively, they do not apologise, practise humility, or recognise irony. So any judgement about acceptance and integration must always be tempered by this knowledge. It's a fragile business. If we Brits send house prices soaring too high or rising unemployment is linked to our struggling legions of self-employed artisans and some despot leapfrogs the democratic safety barriers, no matter how accepted you feel in your adopted country, as an ex-pat you are always vulnerable.

Hopefully, it will never come to that. Hopefully, you will get along just fine with your bemused and amused neighbours. Hopefully, they will bless the day that you moved in to light up the community.

'How important is it to speak the language?'

There are few things worse in life than witnessing a bombastic Englishman trying to make Johnny Frenchman understand what he is trying to say to him by RAISING HIS VOICE AND REPEATEDLY ATTEMPTING TO ENUNCIATE A PHRASE HE LEARNED IN PRIMARY SCHOOL.

If you desire some kind of acceptance in the local community, at the very least you need to make some kind of effort to speak the language. Easier said than done, perhaps: we Brits are lazy swine when it comes to foreign tongues, because English has been a global Esperanto for years. The trouble is, the French are fiercely proud of their poetic language (and refuse to accept the heretical concept that there are roughly four times as many words in the English dictionary as there are in the French one) and equally poor at other ones. They probably speak more English than they sometimes let on and no doubt secretly enjoy making us struggle, but they genuinely appreciate it when we try to speak their language. It's not unreasonable. This is their country.

Things have changed a little of late. Once parliamentarians had woken up to the disturbing realisation that their English was lousy, and that if they still hoped to be world-players, they really ought to address the situation, a kind of shockwave rippled out from Paris. It is more common now to find people eager to air a few words of English to demonstrate their modernity.

You simply miss out on so much of the experience if you don't speak at least rudimentary French. I have a couple of friends who moved over here from Ireland to open an art gallery. She speaks good French and, after only two years, was seen as a pillar of the local community. He, however, is no linguist and feels that he is too old to learn a new language. So he hides away in his studio. If he ventures out, he rarely ventures out alone. He's quite happy, but then he admitted to me that he'd be just as happy back in Ireland.

No, it isn't easy to master a new language. I underestimated the task when we moved over here. Because I was the only boy in my year to achieve a grade-one French

'O' level, I thought I was the cat's pyjamas. Then, as soon as the old man across the road spoke to me in his heavy Corrézian dialect, the panic bells sounded and I realised that my qualification wasn't worth the diploma it was copper-plated on. And when my other, equally aged, neighbour, with a cleft palate to boot, started gesticulating and gibbering about the stones I was digging up in our garden (they served, I discovered, as a rudimentary soak-away for our primitive *fosse septique*), I was frozen to the spot.

But just how do you learn this wretched language? A lot depends on your preferred learning style. There are plenty of good CD-rom and audiotape packages on the market. Some find it better to sign up for a formal course (and the local *chambre de commerce et d'industrie* can act as a broker) or informal conversation group. Others work better with a one-to-one tutor. My pal in Brittany befriended a local builder and offered his services in return for the chance to speak French all day long and, in the process, hone his own building skills. French radio and television can be demoralising: the speed at which they talk can leave you feeling machine-gunned, but a certain amount will get through. I learned a fair amount from sub-titled films and the adventures of TinTin, Asterix and Lucky Luke (the cowboy who draws faster than his shadow).

But there's no substitute for having a go. Forget about the grammar and just get your hands dirty. Don't be afraid to make mistakes. Pedants will relish the opportunity to correct you and others will smile kindly and try to work out what the hell you're attempting to stay. Of course, it can lead to some mortifying moments: like the time I asked the retired teacher next door whether her breasts were growing well at the bottom of the garden (well, *poitrine* and *potiron* are deceptively close). Left alone in our village when my wife and daughter would take off to Cumbria to visit my mother-in-law, my brain would be clinically dead by the end of a day's communication with the locals. I would sleep like a cat after a serial mouse-hunt, but my French would come on in leaps and bounds.

Whichever way you choose to learn your adopted language, be sure to set your sights at a realistic level. There will be some who can achieve fluency, while many will remain merely competent. There's nothing wrong with that, provided you don't frustrate yourself by constantly striving for an unattainable level. If your French is good enough to allow you to participate actively in communal life, even if you never lose that telltale British accent (which many will find quite charming, anyway), then accept it with equanimity. I felt that my French found its natural level several years ago. I stopped listening to Paul Daniels' irritating tapes and gave up TinTin to spend my precious leisure time on rather weightier literature. I can shop and converse at a dinner party and even cope with the telephone; that will do me fine. They say that the acid test is whether or not you dream in your adopted language. To the best of my knowledge, I did once – and I dreamed that I was speaking it badly.

'What about schooling?'

Children are one very good reason for opting to live in France. It's simply a great place to bring up kids. Yes, it can be difficult to find a suitable play group or informal means of support when you first arrive, but there is plenty of state provision available: most small towns have some kind of municipal crèche, which is open during working hours and staffed by trained and registered personnel; and there are so many *assistantes maternelles* (1,500 currently in the Corrèze alone – and still not enough to handle demand) that it becomes a popular topic of conversation among parents. Which *nourrice* (or '*nounou*' to use the affectionate vernacular) do you send your child to? It's a good question because these women – and I have never heard of a man offering his services in this field – can be autocratic potentates with their own theories of child-management that brook no parental interference. Official registration demands

120 hours of training over two years, but choose with discernment and handle with care. The service is state-sponsored in so far as the expense qualifies for tax relief. So, unless you are paying income tax, it can be a pricey option.

Children are encouraged to go to school from about the age of two-and-a-bit – provided that they're *propre* (potty-trained). It seems sometimes indecently young and I well remember the heart-rending moment when I dropped off our daughter at the nearby *école maternelle* (nursery) the first time. She made such a courageous effort not to cry that I almost cried myself. But, for the first two or three years, you can choose whether or not to send them every day of the week, for full days or half days. If your child stays a full day, he or she will be subjected to enforced siestas after lunch until *grand section* (the last year of nursery education), because even the youngest French children invariably stay up until 10.00pm or later.

Anyone who has seen the wonderful documentary film, *Être et Avoir*, about a tiny village school somewhere in the wilds of the Massif Central, will appreciate that some of these rural schools can be very small, with pupils of different ages and different levels working together in a single classroom under the watchful eye of a single teacher. You will also appreciate that French school children work hard: although they're not supposed to be given homework until a certain age, such are the demands of the national curriculum that most teachers will assign it fairly regularly. And although there is a national curriculum (which just about sets out what every child in France will be eating on Tuesdays and reading on Friday afternoons), the standard of education is obviously dependent on the quality of the teacher. (By the same token, the standard of food in the canteen – although generally higher than in the UK, unless Jamie Oliver's campaign ever has a really widespread impact – is dependent on the individual who cooks it.)

The progression through the system is fairly logical and easy to understand. The academic year is roughly the same as it is in the UK, running from the beginning of September to the end of June. However, the year of your child's entry into the system is determined by the calendar year rather than the academic year in which the birthday falls. All children born in 1994, say, will be in the same school year. For example, our own daughter was born in November, which makes her one of the youngest in her class. In the UK, she would be in the year below – and one of the oldest in her class.

Nursery education is open to all children from the age of three to six (*petite*, *moyenne* and *grande sections*). Many schools will accept potty-trained children from the age of two, provided that the school offers a *toute petite section*. Although theoretically voluntary for the first couple of years, around 90 per cent of three-year olds attend *école maternelle*. For working parents, it's a great service, since nursery and primary schools also provide *garderie* facilities to look after children before and after school.

Primary education happens between the ages of 6 and 11. In the rural community, the tiny schools are often grouped together for savings of scale in a *regroupement*, so the primary school may well be located in another village. Nevertheless, if your child has already attended *école maternelle*, he or she will be enrolled automatically at the *école primaire*. This includes the *cours primaire*, the *cours elementaire* (levels 1 and 2) and the *cours moyen* (levels 1 and 2). Put like this, it seems quite logical, though I never managed to get my head round the inevitable abbreviations. This is an incredibly demanding phase of a child's education. In CP, for example, children have to more or less learn to read and write before Christmas – making some of the mechanical exercises they perform during *école maternelle* seem suddenly cunningly clever.

Days are long (from 08.30 to 16.30, not counting journey times, with the obligatory two hours for lunch), and the curriculum is extremely demanding. On many days, our daughter would get home feeling wiped out – but still have to tackle her *devoirs* (homework). During primary education, a child learns the 'three Rs', the rules of grammar and more besides. Frequently, Tilley would have to learn whole poems. With hindsight, this seems less futile and sadistic than it did at the time: an exercise, I now appreciate, to develop memory.

Collège comes next on the agenda. Confusingly, children start secondary education at *sixième* level. Knowing – as you no doubt do already – that the French do most things in a diametrically opposite way to us, it won't surprise you to learn that they work back from the *onzième* (*cours primaire*) to the *première* level and then *terminale*, at which point they sit their *baccalauréat* exams. *Collège* involves a change of building and possibly location, lasts from age 11 to age 15, and concludes with a generic set of exams called the *brevet* (roughly equivalent of our GCSE exams). A national curriculum is followed throughout the country, but there is a choice of modern languages. If your local *collège* doesn't offer a suitable choice, you can request that your child attends a different establishment. However, it's not possible to change for this reason after the first year.

Half way through the *troisième* level, you will be asked to fill in an inevitable form, which indicates your child's intended route through the next tier of the education system. Depending on *brevet* results and the decision of the powers-that-be, your child will go down either a vocational route (and enter a *lycée professionelle*) or a more general route (and enter a *lycée normale* – or *générale et technologique* to give it its full title). Whereas the former are geared up towards vocational qualifications that prepare for and lead into some kind of chosen profession, the latter culminate in some kind of *bac*. Your child will opt for a certain type from the variety on offer, which dictates the courses followed in the final school years and the eventual route through higher education.

University education is certainly not synonymous here with the kind of hedonistic social life that was almost taken as read in my day (you know, a 'broader education' as it was euphemistically termed). For a start, French students don't tend to go to the furthest points of the country in order to get away from their awful parents, but often stay somewhere close enough to the family home that they can get back at weekends. No one with a *bac* pass is refused a university education, but the first year and the ensuing exams are so hard that many students drop out of the equation. If you get through, it's very much noses to the grindstone by the sound of it until you get your degree.

Uppermost in many parents' deliberations about whether to live in France will be the issue of their children's adaptability. When we moved out, our daughter was only ten months old. So it wasn't an issue. Nevertheless, when she went to school for the first time, apparently she remained silent for a good month or two – presumably while she soaked up this strange language that she didn't hear much in the family home – before proudly blurting out her first sentences in French. After that, there was no stopping her; it wasn't that long before she was completely bilingual. Young children have a remarkable capacity to learn and to adapt to change: greater, perhaps, than we give them credit for. However, it must be a very daunting prospect for a twelve-year old, say, to find himself or herself in a class where everyone – teacher and classmates – is speaking in an unintelligible tongue. I have a French friend here whose job is to provide supplementary tuition to children such as British *immigrés* who are having problems with the language. And I know a fair number of teenagers who have coped pretty well with the ordeal. If it proves too much of an ordeal, then there is always the possibility of *redoublement*. Inevitably, the idea of repeating a year has a certain stigma attached to it and parents objecting to the school's decision have the right to appeal. However, for a child coming from the UK and experiencing problems with the transition, it seems like a pragmatic option.

Generally speaking, I think that the education system here is better than it is in the UK. Whenever we have felt at all negative about the French experience, we have consoled ourselves with this thought. We couldn't face going back for the very reason that our daughter seemed happy at school and the knowledge that, without the funds to buy a good private education for her, she would be better off here. Somehow, the French system seems to have found a kind of balance between respecting their charges as developing human beings and imposing a disciplined framework within which they can develop. *Education civique* (social responsibility) is part of the curriculum here. It might be slightly old-fashioned and you could argue that British kids are more individual than their rather more regulated French equivalents, but I know which ones are better behaved and less intimidating *en masse*. As I say, the system works its children hard: the final baccalaureate is definitely worth its weight in parchment and never, unlike A levels, subject to sniping about diminishing value.

'*What should I know about other public services?*'

Apart from the very occasional visit to a local doctor, my wife fully encountered the French health service for the first time on Christmas morning, 2005. We had just finished opening our presents and I moved from the tree to the kitchen area in order to make our traditional Christmas-morning coffee (the one that comes festooned with holly berries). Remembering a final present for our daughter that she had left on the back seat of the 205, Deborah nipped out in her dressing gown and slippers to retrieve this apparently vital gift, slipped on the frosty ground and put out her right arm to break her fall. She broke her arm somewhere near the shoulder (and of course it had to be the right arm: her principal means of winning the family bread). Since I had recently done my back in, we had to telephone a friend and ask her to abandon her festivities in order to take Deborah to the hospital in Brive. After a brief wait, she was bandaged up and lodged in an excessively hot if comfortable room with one other patient for three days. Although she wasn't allowed to eat initially in case the break necessitated an operation, she saw the Christmas Day menu: pâté de foie gras, coquilles St. Jacques, capon and a chocolate log. Anathema, of course, for a vegetarian like her, but indicative of the prevalent catering standards.

After hospital, district nurses would visit on a daily basis to change the bandages that I obtained from the local *pharmacie* by means of her precious green *Carte Vitale*. This was followed by a programme of re-education with a *kinésthérapeute* (physiotherapist) in a nearby town. After two months, and thanks also to daily home massage with essential oils, she was back at the coal-face faster than you could say Jacques Reurbeenssen.

The health service here is modern, efficient, hygienic and amply funded. But it's not free. Although Deborah handed over her *Carte Vitale* to the hospital admin staff and, hey presto, her bill was paid with a swipe, remember that she pays exorbitant *cotisations* to cover such things as medical insurance. Nor is that cover 100 per cent. She also has to take out a private top-up insurance for all the hidden extras. This doesn't come cheap. The premium varies, of course, depending on age, general health and extent of cover. Back in 2007, Waldemar Kaminski, an insurance broker based in south-west France who provides an English-speaking service for ex-pats, suggested the following figures for clients in a reasonable state of health, seeking basic top-up cover: for a young couple of around 26 with two small children, quotes ranged from €75 to €95 per month; for a middle-aged couple in their late 40s with a child aged 12, quotes ranged from €75 to €95 per month; for a retired couple aged around 70, quotes ranged from €92 to €140 per month. For 'reasonable cover' (which would include a private room in hospital), you had to add around €25 per month to the minimum and maximum figures quoted.

We'll look at the practical business of arranging medical insurance and registering with your local doctor in the last chapter of the book. At this stage, all you probably need to know is that the health service, although expensive, is excellent. Surprise, surprise it's also rather rigid. Alternative or complementary therapies exist, but are not reimbursed (as visits, say, to a GP are) and are constantly under attack from the official medical mafia. If pharmaceutical medication is what you're after, you couldn't come to a better country. The French are obsessed to the point of mania by pills and sachets. (And perhaps their ongoing love affair with suppositories might help explain a characteristic stiffness and correctness.) Every pill issued seems to come with two or three others to counteract the undesirable side effects of the original prescription.

I once witnessed the incredible cocktail of medication consumed on a daily basis by the wife of an overbearing Parisian, who holidayed in our old village. It was just before or just after their midday meal. She took from her handbag one range of pills after another, dropped each one onto her plate till she resembled a gambler at a casino riding a wave of good fortune, then washed them all down with a glass of Evian. I could only stare in stupefaction and contemplate the secondary health problems triggered by such a toxic mixture.

One soon learns here that the French are a nation of inveterate hypochondriacs. So rest assured that health is very high on the agenda. At the same time, they don't like opening their purses wider than they must. Therefore, because dentistry is only partially covered by their insurance, the state of the national mouth is on the whole not good. A shame, really, because I have generally found French dentists to be very good and cheaper (even without any insurance) than UK dentists still operating under the NHS.

Other public services – gas, electricity, water, telephone and so on – are much-of-a-muchness: big, impersonal and not especially efficient. I would, though, like to put in a word for the library service, which is a joy. In the Corrèze, for example, we were visited each month by a *bibliobus*, which, for many of the older people in the village, was akin to a trip to the theatre. They would wait by the fountain for its arrival, then spend a good half hour or so on board, chatting to the driver and his 'charming female assistant', before booking out their reading matter for another month. In addition to this, there was an excellent *Centre Culturel* in nearby Tulle, where you could attend recitals and concerts, and borrow books, videos, DVDs and CDs from staff so obliging and helpful that you wondered whether they could possibly be civil servants. There was always money for new acquisitions and they would often respond to your own suggestions. I left the area with a heavy heart, thinking this was something unique to the town. Then, one morning, I wandered into the central library in Brive and found something fit for a capital city. It has satisfied my exorbitant needs ever since. The culture may be different here, but they place a high value on it.

'If we go for this option, what should we do with our house in the UK?'

This is where my wife and I always agree to disagree. She felt that the £60,000 we received for our four-bedroom terraced house in Sheffield was a good price. I can't help thinking about the tens of thousands that would have accrued had we let the house to long-term tenants. She argues that we might not have stayed the course if we'd had the UK safety net that the house would have represented – and perhaps she's right on that score. Perhaps it makes you lazy if you come out here with the attitude that 'we can always go back if it doesn't work out'. However, we know that we can only ever go back if we are prepared to swap our house and land for, say, a two-up two-down with back yard and outside loo in Middlesbrough.

So – to let or to sell, that is the question? UK property is no longer the best investment on the market. Most people I know who have moved here with a property back home have eventually sold it. Even with the best agent in the world, letting can be a headache and distance only exacerbates the problems. Moreover, to sell releases the capital for home improvements and gets the mortgage monkey off your back. And who knows? Your first experience of buying in France might prove so positive that you want to do it again.

SUMMARY

France is potentially a great place in which to buy a house – but owning property here can bring with it a whole new set of potential problems. Although it will often work out fine, there's also a chance that it could all go horribly wrong. So ask yourself:

- ✔ **What's my motivation for buying here? Am I perhaps romanticizing the whole notion?**
- ✔ **Does it have to be France – as opposed to, say, Spain, Italy or Bulgaria?**
- ✔ **If I want to buy as a pure investment, have I thought about the various legal and fiscal implications?**
- ✔ **If I buy a holiday home, am I sure I want to spend all my holidays in the same place – often working on the house for the duration?**
- ✔ **If I'm buying to live here permanently, have I really thought through the associated issues?**
  - How will I support myself?
  - How easy will it be to find work?
  - How might it affect my partner: is he or she really committed to the same dream?
  - How will I manage without family and friends?
  - If I'm moving from a city, how easy will it be to adapt to rural life?
  - Have I considered what it might be like in winter?
  - Will I be accepted as part of the local community?
  - How will I cope with the language?
  - Have I thought about schooling?
  - Have I thought about other public services?
  - What will I do with my house in the UK?

Chapter 2. *Where in France should I look for a house?*

To us Brits, France seems like a very big country. To my Canadian friend, brought up in the wilds of British Columbia, it seems pretty tiny. Whatever your perspective, the fact is that France is the biggest country in Western Europe. Its population is similar to that of the UK and most of that is concentrated in certain urban zones. Arriving here from our busy overcrowded island, the predominant impression is that of open space, fresh air and a green and pleasant countryside. Drive through somewhere like the Creuse, for instance – a *département* denuded by the carnage of two world wars and the drift to the cities in search of employment – and you can cruise for miles without passing a car.

Being such a comparatively large country, there is, of course, a rich variety of landscape, property characteristics and climate. I never cease to marvel at how *much* variety and how *much* beauty is on offer. For that reason, it's worth exploring further than the first area in which you stop and with which, almost inevitably, you fall in love. So I offer the following brief survey of the 21 regions into which the 93 mainland *départements* have been grouped for economic and administrative convenience. Corsica represents the 22nd region. It is a stunning island, but I have decided to omit it on the grounds that the vast majority of you will be thinking of looking at property on the mainland. What follows is a highly subjective, thoroughly opinionated survey based on a combination of research and my own experience. It is no substitute for a visit, but may save you a little time in deciding where you might care to visit.

Q *'What should I know about Alsace?'*

The industrial north east of France is one of the cheapest areas in which to buy property, but prices in Alsace are higher than average for this part of France. This no doubt reflects the unusually good employment opportunities and the proximity to the administrative centre of Strasbourg (which has, I'm told, a big young population). It's an important wine-growing region and the landscape, bordered as it is by the Vosges Mountains and the Rhine valley, befits the indigenous half-timbered stone houses. I'm told that it's particularly attractive in the autumn. However, the steep-pitched roofs point to fairly severe winters.

Munster cheese comes from Alsace and it tastes rather better than its uncommonly pungent smell. Generally, however, the area is too industrialised and too near to the German border for my taste. Indeed, certain local laws are based on German law. It's hard enough to come to terms with the singularities of the French without having to figure out the quirks of the Alsatian character, dialect and legal system.

Q 'What should I know about Aquitaine?'

This is the largest of the French regions and contains not only the *département* of the Dordogne, but also that of the Pyrénées-Atlantiques (which includes the lovely Pays Basque), and therefore gets my vote as a very desirable place to live. Though the *département* of the Landes seems chiefly made up of mile upon mile of geometric pine forests, planted to stabilise the coastal sand, the 400km coastline boasts some of the finest beaches in Christendom – sand so soft that it squeaks underfoot, stretching as far as the eye can see and washed by a dramatic sea that is understandably popular with surfers. Around Bordeaux (a famously elegant city, now with a new super-modern tram system to help alleviate some of the traditional traffic problems), the stony land is devoted to serried ranks of vines, while much of the rolling countryside to the south (and to the east of the pine forests) is a rich market-gardening area. The fact that melons are one of the main crops suggests that the climate is suitably mild. House prices are a healthy average and the only thing not in its favour is that the Dordogne is synonymous with the kind of stereotypical wine-sipping leisured ex-pat from whom I, for one, would run a mile.

Q 'What should I know about the Auvergne?'

Once, when our daughter was two years old, we decided to trace a lunatic route across the Auvergne and, indeed, the very centre of France to visit an old friend in the Alps. It was an eye-opener. For a start, the journey seemed interminable. What's more, it crossed some of the most starkly beautiful scenery I had – up until then – encountered. The Auvergne represents the granite heart of this great country, but you'll find more life in the dormant volcanoes of the Puy de Dôme. In the winter, it can be as bleak as the scattered unwelcoming farms and colder than the Klondike in a blizzard. Ex-pats hardened by Bodmin, Dartmoor or the Highlands of Scotland would have the keenest chance of surviving all the year round. Bearing in mind, too, that is one of the most depopulated areas in Europe, you would also need to make your own entertainment. Clermont-Ferrand has a certain Sheffield-like quality that has always appealed to me. But if a town like Montluçon is the second biggest cultural centre, you would have to be either a diehard pioneer or a 'contrarian' to move here.

However… in summer, when the sun softens its edges, the region can be very beautiful. It boasts real mountains, the dramatic gorges of some mighty rivers, some of the least spoilt countryside you could track down anywhere in the world and property that's still (in some corners) as cheap as the proverbials. As a place to get away from it all (with potentially no neighbours for miles around), it could be a great bet for a holiday home.

Q 'What should I know about Basse-Normandie?'

This area will be familiar to anyone who has ever driven south from or north to the Channel ports of Caen or Cherbourg. That's part of the trouble, in fact: visitors are usually on their way to somewhere else. Which is a shame, because charming ports like Honfleur, elegant seaside resorts like Deauville and Trouville, the stunning 'one-off' that is Mont St-Michel (which seems to rise out of the sea like a cross between some Arthurian castle and an intergalactic rocket), and the wooded hilly area to the south of the region known (somewhat fancifully) as Swiss Normandy are all worthy of a few days' tour. Personally, I'd tend to leave it there. Great, perhaps (given the affordable property and cross-Channel travel links), for a regular seaside retreat, but I can't quite see the point of living somewhere that's so near and so similar to the south coast of England. Isn't it, after all, nicknamed 'Lower Kent'? Besides, it's dangerously close to the French nuclear power industry's uranium processing plant at the tip of the Cherbourg peninsular.

Q 'What should I know about Bourgogne?'

In brief, this region is rural, not too far from Paris but quite off the beaten track, mercifully by-passed by the Autoroute du Soleil while criss-crossed by rivers and canals, renowned for its light Burgundy wines, its gastronomy and its Dijon mustard, relatively unexplored by Brits and therefore not short of potential property bargains. East, but not too far east, it is well worth a reconnaissance trip.

Q 'What should I know about Bretagne?'

One of the last great bastions of French Catholicism, Brittany is right out on a limb, geographically and culturally. Some would say that the region has more affinity with Wales, Cornwall and other UK Celtic enclaves than it does with the rest of France. Indeed, Lorient hosts an annual *Festival Interceltique* to which European Celts gather in worrying numbers to enjoy traditional Celtic music and a general knees-up. I prefer to see it as the most worthwhile and sufficiently different of all the areas that are otherwise too near to the UK for my taste.

Lovers of the 1953 film *Monsieur Hulot's Holiday* will be pleased to hear that the coast is still very popular with the holidaying French and with tourists in general. The north coast is reassuringly redolent of somewhere like Dorset; the extreme north west coast is ruggedly beautiful; the more sheltered south coast ushers in the flatter Atlantic coast further below. Property is unsurprisingly cheaper inland than on the coast, but rumours of anti-British sentiment (for invading the region and inflating prices) have filtered down to these parts. These rumours, the notorious nitrate run-offs from the many intensive farms, a lunatic fringe of Breton nationalists, and the cold, damp, windswept winters could combine to ring some alarm bells.

Nevertheless, my ex-'copper' friend (who deliberately chose a wet region in order to harvest rainwater and grow willow commercially) settled with his wife near the lively, thriving university-city of Rennes and they seem to enjoy both the land and its inhabitants. The local education, interestingly, is considered the best in France. And the Ecology Party did better here in the 2002 elections than in any other part of France. A distinct possibility, I would suggest, particularly if you want to learn to speak Breton, hone your green credentials and like cider with your *crêpes*.

Q 'What should I know about Centre?'

It's a shame that the bureaucrats chose to give an area synonymous with the celebrated Loire Valley such an unlovely label. Enough to put a robot off a visit.

Around Chartres, the countryside seems interminably flat and tedious. During summer, the giant irrigation units ceaselessly pump water onto one intensive crop or another. The concrete piers of an abandoned monorail experiment serves as a reminder that legions of Centre commuters make the swift daily journey to Paris and back. There is nothing much to recommend it apart from the twin towers of Chartres cathedral, one of the architectural wonders of the medieval world.

Head south and west of Orléans, though, and more interesting things happen. They say, for example, that the river Loire represents the point beyond which northern France gives way to the south, that the evocative continental chorus of crickets, cicadas and other scratching insects starts here and gets progressively louder the nearer you get to the Mediterranean. The area is studded with fantastical chateaux and carpeted with the kind of elegant deciduous woodland where the gentry traditionally hunted deer. The Loir et Cher *département* (which takes its name from the two lesser rivers that join the Loire) produces some of the best goats' cheese in France. Property is reasonably priced and it's both near enough to and far enough from the Channel to make it attractive to both 'lifers' and holidaymakers.

Q 'What should I know about Champagne-Ardenne?'

Best known for the effervescent white wine imbibed by sophisticates and partygoers, the best that could be said for this region is that it borders in the north the only really scenic part of Belgium. The rural communities are still fairly poor and primitive. Property prices are correspondingly low and reflect the fact that dreary crops like cabbage and sugar beet are grown in abundance, that winters are worryingly cold, wet and windy, and that – not unsurprisingly – it is not a favoured location for second homes. Despite the fact that the new TGV *Est* link might attract new businesses and more investment in the area, I would prefer to drink champagne somewhere other than the territory in which the grape is grown.

Q 'What should I know about Franche-Comté?'

After reading Stendhal's classic *The Scarlet and Black*, this region became high on the family visiting list. Sandwiched between the Vosges in the north, the Jura in the south and Switzerland in the east, it is glorious: a land of lakes and forests and river gorges and picturesque villages with their distinctive houses and domed bell towers. The Jura mountains are lovely: less majestic perhaps than the Alps but more domestic. Moreover, property is considerably more affordable and could offer an excellent investment opportunity. Comté cheese is damn fine, too.

Q 'What should I know about Haute-Normandie?'

My comments about Basse-Normandie apply – to a degree. The fact, however, that the area is so popular with British second-homers indicates that it has rather more to offer. Not only the ferry links to the UK via Dieppe and (the rather grim) Le Havre (which, as France's second largest port, was subject to extensive bombing during the Second World War), but also a beautiful coast studded with lovely seaside towns like Le Tréport and Etretat and a verdant hinterland of apple orchards and rolling pasture land. Rouen, the last major port before Paris, serves as a busy if rather too industrial centre and boasts a cathedral painted under every imaginable light by Claude Monet. In fact, coast and hinterland are redolent of the Impressionists and Post-Impressionists, who could have travelled here from Paris in search of subjects without very much difficulty. Significantly, Monet chose to settle in the region and created his renowned water garden at Giverny.

The traditional architecture features the distinctive chocolate-box pretty *colombage* houses, with their criss-cross pattern of exposed beams. Accordingly, though, average prices are rather higher than their Basse-Normandie equivalents.

Q 'What should I know about Paris/Ile de France?'

Unsurprisingly, this – along with Provence and the Côte d'Azur – is the most expensive area in France in which to buy property. It's also the most densely populated area, so there's not much available unless you've got some serious money. But, speaking as a Londoner who would never contemplate a *pied à terre* there, I would – if I had the means – jump at the chance of owning a weekend apartment in, say, Montmartre. Paris is a beautiful city: it's cosmopolitan, elegant, vibrant and, for all the talk of the wild, violent *banlieues*, a lot less threatening (to my mind, anyway) than London. However, unless you're moving over for the purpose of employment, it might be best to avoid an overcrowded property market.

As for the environs of Paris, having got hopelessly lost with my brother in a car in the vicinity of Versailles and having seen too many news reports of tension in the *banlieues*, I wouldn't give them the time of day.

Q 'What should I know about Languedoc-Roussillon?'

The more acceptable face of both the Mediterranean and the Massif Central. With its distinctly Spanish influence and balmy climate, this is a region whose population is rising as steeply as its property prices – and in recent years something like 75 per cent of property purchases here have involved British buyers. However, it's a big region and you are more likely to find some bargains away from the coast in some of the comparatively unexplored parts like such Division 2 wine-growing areas as the Aude, rocky Corbière and the gorgeous valley of the Herault.

Montpellier is the biggest and liveliest city of the region. Its population swells by around 1,000 new inhabitants per month and is expected to double by 2030 – but it does appear to have a reputation for violence. Travelling north from the city on the motorway in the direction of Clermont-Ferrand, you cross some suitably wild and empty stretches of the *massif*, which nevertheless seem rather more habitable because of their proximity to the Med. East of Montpellier, the coast meanders about in search of the Camargues. West of Montpellier, it takes you to the charming port of Sète and then drifts off aimlessly until it reaches the traditional artists' colony of Collioure, just beyond which the Pyrenees sweep dramatically down to the sea. Had I been shrewd, I would have bought an inexpensive little apartment for holiday lets when I first saw the place quite a few years ago. Alas, I denied us an excellent return on a hypothetical investment.

Carcassonne (despite its busy airport) is reputedly one of the loveliest towns in France. I saw it once from the *autoroute*: its battlements glowing dusky pink against a backdrop of the *Montagnes Noires*. It's just one of the delights of a region that has a lot going for itself. Since my car door was nearly ripped off its hinges while stopping for a 'comfort break' in the Corbière hills, I would have to say that only the wild winds which howl down from the mountains would make me think twice about settling here.

45

Q 'What should I know about Limousin?'

The Limousin is ancient, traditional, rural and still affordable. The Haute-Vienne is empty, the Corrèze is emptier still and the Creuse is so empty that even the French sometimes forget it's there. Roughly a third of the region is covered in thick deciduous and/or pine forests. To tempt people here, they made the A20 toll-free and even advertised once for British farmers to come and tend their ginger-brown Limousin cows.

The Corrèze, in my opinion, is the most attractive of the three *départements*, partly because the landscape is dotted with some of the loveliest and most ancient villages in France. The Haute-Vienne is fine, but somehow characterised by the sombre city of Limoges. It's no doubt pure coincidence, but it always seems to be raining whenever I pass through it. The Creuse (hollow) is the approximate geographical centre of the country and it's as if the life-blood has flowed away with the rivers that traverse it. Undeniably pretty and graced by the gorgeous Lac de Vassivière, it's maybe best suited to hermits and misanthropes.

Despite the erstwhile unstoppable rise in prices throughout the south-western Corrèze, this is still apparently the cheapest part of France for property hunters. With its lakes, rivers, woodland and wildlife, the region is a nature-lover's paradise. But a word in your ear. It took me a fair few years to figure out why the Corrèze is known as the *pays vert* (the green country). It's green because, like Ireland, it can rain. It can rain and rain and rain.

Q 'What should I know about Lorraine?'

Well, the traditional quiche comes from Lorraine, but that's no reason for owning a house in the region. We've met many settlers from Metz and Nancy (the two principal cities) in the Corrèze – and you have to ask the question 'why?' I once read an article that featured some picturesque rivers and canals around Metz, and the Vosges Mountains form a natural divide in the south-east, but the region is largely industrial and features the vast Saar coalfield. Besides, Verdun is one of the principal towns in Lorraine. Virtually every French village I have ever visited features a war memorial with the names of the fallen engraved in the stone. Long lists of young men, many with the same surname. Most of them would have died for the glory of France at Verdun. I dare say it's a pleasant enough town these days, but owning a house anywhere in the vicinity would be like building your dream home next to Dachau.

Q 'What should I know about Midi-Pyrénées'

We made our home in the Lot, which is one of the eight *départements* of this big and varied region. So please forgive me if you detect a little bias.

To be honest, although the Lot is (understandably) very popular with the British, the rugged limestone *causse* (or plateau) that separates the lush valleys of the Dordogne and the Lot can be rather stark and arid. It suggests, too, a worrying shortage of rain, though this is not, as yet, a problem in the river valleys.

Further south and east lie some long-buried treasures of the Aveyron. Part of it, as befits the Massif Central, is wild and windswept – and now boasts the extraordinary viaduct that carries the motorway over the valley of the Tarn and the former bottleneck of Millau. The valley of the eponymous river, however, is distinctly Corrézian, featuring steep-sided densely wooded valleys and impossibly picturesque villages, some of which appear to teeter on top of outcrops of the indigenous granite. Cordes sur Ciel, for example, gets my vote as the loveliest village in France.

The Tarn has long been a popular location for British ex-pats and owners of second homes. It features beautiful fortified *bastide* villages and individual houses (often built around a central courtyard), the ancient red-brick towns of Gaillac and Albi, and a gorge that's a distant cousin of the Grand Canyon.

The Gers is a land of rolling farmland that benefits from a proximity to Toulouse. *La Ville Rose* is a warm (in both senses) and prosperous city whose shops, restaurants, cultural variety and general animation reflect a huge student population. Almost enough to tempt me back out of the countryside.

Until recently, I had always cited Savoie as my favourite part of France. Then I discovered Béarne and Haute Béarne (now lumped together as Hautes Pyrénées): lush wooded valleys set against a majestic mountain backdrop.

When you think that the climate (despite surprisingly harsh winters in certain parts) is generally better than average and property prices are still somehow lower than the national average, it adds up to an attractive package.

Q *'What should I know about Nord Pas-de-Calais?'*

So far north, so far east and so industrial that you might as well live in Belgium – and I fail to see how that would benefit anyone's quality of life.

The old centre of the biggest city, Lille, is rather lovely, but it's significant that many of the Lillists who holidayed at the lake near our former home (bought and maintained for the city's careworn populace) renounced the attractions of France's fourth largest city for the rustic splendours of the Corrèze.

Where once it was cloth and textiles, and then mining and steel, these days it's the car, transport, IT and communications industries that breathe economic life into the region. This relative prosperity would seem to account for the fact that property is not as cheap as it should be. The best I can say about the region is that the proximity to Channel ports and the Eurostar junction at Lille offers an easy escape route back to the UK for anyone compelled to settle here.

On the other hand, if you want to settle or own a second home in a seaside town with a name like Berck, this is the region for you.

Q *'What should I know about Pays de la Loire?'*

On paper, this sounds like a really good bet. Tucked protectively under Brittany and Normandy, the region is, like Centre, far enough from La Manche to make it worth the effort of moving from the UK, while near enough to the Channel ports to make journeys to and from a holiday home not too much of an endurance test. Around 350km of Atlantic coastline is an obvious attraction.

As the name would suggest, the region is dominated by the classic valley of the Loire, with its vineyards, fairy-tale chateaux, gentle landscape, mild climate and such elegant prosperous towns as Angers and Saumur. It is known as 'the garden of France' for good reason.

The valley of the Sarthe reputedly has similar charms on offer. Although I've always given its principal town, Le Mans, a wide berth, it has plenty of things going for it: ample employment opportunities, general economic health, a rapid TGV link to Paris and, somewhat incongruously, a reputation as France's leading gay-friendly metropolis.

The cognoscenti have long raved about the Vendée, which tempts tourists with miles of sandy beaches and a particularly sunny microclimate. The Loire Atlantique to its north is rather more industrial, though I'm told that Nantes is well worth the effort.

Seaside, pleasant landscape, mild climate, easy travel links, property prices below the national average, better-than-normal employment opportunities. Tempting.

Q *'What should I know about Picardie?'*

A river, the Somme, runs through it. After all the aerial bombardments and the Germans' scorched-earth retreat behind the Hindenburg Line, it's hard to believe that Picardie can support anything other than poppies. Yet once more there are crops, cows, people and, one imagines, the blooming roses of legend.

Maybe the massed letting of blood accounts for the richness of the soil. Grain and vegetables are cultivated intensively across a relentlessly flat landscape over which speed Eurostar trains and Eurolines coaches. Though I've paused at the outlandish chateau of Chantilly in the rather more rolling southern part of the region, I plead guilty to never having investigated Amiens' legendary gothic cathedral. The estuary of the Somme is popular with bird watchers and the sailing fraternity, and the region does indeed seem fairly unspoilt. Property is cheaper than average, but the area is so sombre and too redolent for me of all those ghosts of a tragic past.

Q 'What should I know about Poitou-Charentes?'

To my mind, the principal attraction is the region's Atlantic coastline and a unique marshy hinterland known as the Marais. The nearest equivalent, I suppose, to England's Norfolk Broads, this is a green and peaceful lattice of fields and ancient canals.

The port of La Rochelle is probably the jewel in the regional crown: beautiful, bourgeois, busy – and bleedin' expensive! A modern suspension bridge links it to the Ile de Ré, beloved of celebrities like Charles Aznavour and politicians like Lionel Jospin. We spent three disappointingly wet days on the island with half the French population looking for something to do in their cars.

The inland *départements* are, in my book, nothing too much to write home about. Vienne is rural and pleasant, but a kind of second-division Haute Vienne. Rich in history, the administrative capital of Poitiers has cleverly seduced visitors to the area by creating a concrete theme park (Futuroscope) dedicated to the technology of the future.

The Charente is popular with the Brits and the indigenous houses, with their Roman-tiled roofs and sandy pink walls, are simple and attractive. The landscape is rolling and heavily planted with vines for cognac and other local specialities. Angoulême is its urban focus. It's a pleasant enough old place, which houses an annual festival of cartoon art, but I always get lost there, bewildered by signposts that leave you wondering what on earth happened to your destination.

Nevertheless, the climate is agreeable and property prices are towards the lower end of the scale. I'm not totally smitten. But who am I to put you off?

Q 'What should I know about Provence-Alpes-Côte d'Azur?'

Principally that you need to be rich to live there. Property prices are about as high as you can get in France.

The average price is no doubt bumped up by the property along the coast, east of Marseilles. By contrast with the tranquillity of the Camargues to the west of France's dynamic (and slightly scary) third city, the Côte d'Azur is infernal: too many cars, too many people, too many houses, not enough space. It's little wonder, as certain estate agents have told me, that lovers of a quieter life are selling up and moving to the south-west.

Inland, it's a different matter. The Alpes Maritimes and Provence are both lovely, though the latter has been well scoured now by property hunters in search of the Holy Mayle and his promised land. Heading north via the photogenic lavender fields you reach Alpes-de-Haute-Provence and then the Hautes Alpes, which are both inspiring. A few years ago, I toyed with the idea of Briançon in the north-east corner of the region, tempted by its sunshine boast. When I thought about it more rationally, I considered how the snow lingers for months. The experience of trying to fit chains to the car one bitterly cold winter's night in the middle of a blizzard on an unlit Alpine pass left me feeling humiliated and close to tears. If you can afford a holiday chalet or an apartment in the mountains, there must be good prospects for letting the property most of the year round. But the area demands a certain feeling for snow.

Further west, the Rhône Valley separates the mountains from the Massif Central. The mighty river flows down past the cultural walled city of Avignon to Arles, where it fans out into a massive marshy delta. There's plenty of fruit about and not a little industry and the whole place can be just a little eerie. I've never fortunately experienced a full-blown *mistral*, which whips up or down (or both) this geographical corridor, but I'm sure all those shutters banging in the night would grate on the nerves like a cat scratching on a window pane.

Marseilles, as France's third city, is the biggest conurbation in the region. Stuck in heavy traffic, it seems, whenever I've been there, my ears ringing with the constant blasts of horns, I've consistently failed to notice its many reputed charms. However, the coming of the TGV Méditerrannée has provided a three-hour link to the capital and the heart of the old city is the subject of the largest urban and economic redevelopment project in France. Moreover, it has linked up with Aix-en-Provence, half an hour to the north, which was fairly recently voted as the best place to live in France.

Q *'What should I know about Rhône-Alpes?'*

This is a region of stark contrasts. To the east lies Savoie and Haute-Savoie. Of the two, I prefer Savoie: the mountains are less august, but a little more human in scale. The memory of the evening sun illuminating the rocky face of the Massif de Chartreuse just south of Chambéry will abide with me forever. A recent short break to the Lac du Bourget (France's biggest entirely natural lake) and a tour of Aix-les-Bains underlined why Queen Victoria loved the area and confirmed that Savoy is simply sublime. Moreover, there's a little less snow underfoot, making life without skis in winter more possible.

West of the mountains, however, is that awful Rhône corridor again. You only have to travel south out of Lyon on the *autoroute* that links this great city (France's second city, despite Marseille's annexation of Aix-en-Provence) with the once-great Saint-Étienne to appreciate why unemployment is lower and salaries and property prices are higher than the national averages. It's industry and urban sprawl all the way. Lyon has been called the French Manchester. Its factories and refineries and chemical works belch out fumes round the clock, so it didn't surprise me to discover that the Rhône Valley produces more nuclear power (not to mention nougat) than anywhere else in France.

In a breathtaking situation, surrounded by mountains, Grenoble is another modern industrial centre. Chemicals, pharmaceuticals and nuclear research: *spécialités de la ville*. If it weren't for the signs advising motorway motorists to be more 'zen', you might just want to put your foot down and get out of town.

The Ardèche is a refreshing change to all this industry. It's a kind of eastern Massif Aveyron-equivalent: sublime scenery, but fairly undiscovered. When we took that crazy epic drive *across* the Massif Central to the Alps, we followed the fabled Route Napoléon from Le Puy through the Ardèche and then down interminably wiggling roads to Valence. It's an impossibly long trip, but the scenery's to die for (or, in the case of my wife and daughter, to sleep through).

I can't think of any other region where the contrast between the ugly and the beautiful is so pronounced, so what more appropriate point to end this potted property-seeker's *tour de France* before we get right down to the real nitty-gritty?

SUMMARY

France is a big, beautiful and very varied country. Each region has its own charms and characteristics. When thinking about where in France to buy your house, you would be well advised to address a number of generic questions:

- ✔ **Is it cheaper or more expensive than average – and why?**
- ✔ **How easy is it to get back and forth to the UK from this region?**
- ✔ **What are the special features of the climate?**
- ✔ **How good or poor are the employment opportunities here?**
- ✔ **What is the nearest foreign country?**
- ✔ **What are the prevalent cultural influences?**
- ✔ **Is it a cosmopolitan or very traditional region?**
- ✔ **Are there many foreigners living here?**
- ✔ **Is it land-locked or does it have a coastline?**
- ✔ **How popular is it with tourists?**
- ✔ **Do the advantages of buying here outweigh the disadvantages?**

Chapter 3. *How do I go about finding the right house?*

Once you've decided where in France you want to live or to spend your holidays, you should then ask yourself a further set of questions about the type of house you want. My friends in Brittany went about it, I think, in the ideal way. First, they took a few weeks off to explore the various regions of France that particularly interested them. When they decided that Brittany's soil and climate would be ideal for their plans, they narrowed down their search to an area within spitting distance of Rennes (because the culture that the city could offer them would be an essential facet of their new life here). Then they rented somewhere in the area and waited until they finally saw the house they'd hoped to find.

Of course, we don't all have the time on our hands to play it this way. Because time is always pressing, there is a danger of making snap decisions. So many get seduced by size: of house, land or both. We fell into exactly the same trap all those years ago. It's understandable. When you're used to something fairly modest back home and you see something much bigger for the same or less money, well you want to grab it. Sometime later, perhaps, you discover that it's too big for your needs, requires too much work and money to keep up and conclude that you were silly buying it in the first place. This set of questions is designed to instil some discipline! To help you really focus your search to make the best use of the limited time available and to ensure that you opt for the house that best suits a defined set of needs.

Q 'Do I want to buy somewhere in the middle of the country or in or near a town?'

To many of us, whether ex-pats or holidaymakers, the 'French experience' is about the feeling of space and the lack of modern hubbub. Whether it's by the sea or by a pool or somewhere in the country, it's about unwinding and taking the time to enjoy some of the simpler pleasures of life. It's

55

unlikely (unless it's for a specific reason, such as a job) that we would go property-hunting in a town or a big city. Many French towns and small cities, though, can be very civilised places and offer buyers a rewarding if different facet of the experience. Property prices tend to be a little higher, but there is a ready market for letting on an all-year-round basis. This can get quite complicated, and we'll look at some of the ins and outs of the procedure in the last chapter, but it could be a viable pure investment option. Besides, if you want to buy somewhere on the coast, a small town or city might be the only possibility.

We looked at some of the drawbacks of living in the middle of the country in Chapter 1: the isolation, the loneliness, the hard winters, the dearth of culture and so on. So why not have your cake and eat it too? Instead of opting for the middle of nowhere, consider a half-way house: somewhere a 15- or 20-minute drive from a lively town where you can do your shopping (at both a supermarket and a weekly market), buy your building materials, go to the bank, find a cinema that shows films in *version originale*, drink coffee and eat out on occasions – and from where you can easily escape. We didn't really think about it much when we bought our farmhouse in the Corrèze (after all, it was originally intended only for holidays), but the proximity to dear old unlovely Tulle proved immensely practical and maybe saved our sanity.

Q *'What are the (dis)advantages of living in a village?'*

There are villages and there are villages. Some are stone dead and you might find yourself living in the same kind of splendid isolation as you would if you bought somewhere in the middle of nowhere. Our old village had one amenity: an old stone fountain from which refreshing spring water trickled day and night (until the day that someone discovered that it passed through an old flaking lead pipe). It served as a focal point for anyone who wanted to congregate, but these days I'd look for something with – at the very least – a *boulangerie* and, preferably, a post office and either a *bar tabac* or a restaurant. Quite apart from the social aspect, holidaymakers renting your property can feel cheated without such facilities. Repeat bookings could be difficult.

The advantages of choosing a village are several. There's the sense of society and looking out for one another. As the owner of a second home, this is particularly important. Disasters occur. And crime happens, even if you're living in the French countryside. Not quite on the same scale as it does in the UK, nevertheless it's reassuring to know that someone will be keeping an eye on your second home during your absence. There will be people nearby to chat to and, no doubt, a handyman to ask for help with a dripping tap, and/or someone with a strimmer who's prepared to slash through your undergrowth, all of which will do wonders for your French and your social standing (provided you remember the cautionary tale of Madame X and her breasts growing at the foot of her garden, and keep the gaffes respectable).

Of course, some of these aspects can serve as double-edged swords. The closeness of village life can mean that you'll be spending far too much time chatting or listening to someone's plaints (when you just want to be quiet), either accepting or reciprocating invitations to *boire un aperitif* (although you could consider this a plus), or exposing yourself to the sort of small-minded mentality that transforms your business into their business. If you have small children or animals, you have to remember that a narrow country road through a sleepy village is still an integral part of a racetrack for the sort of maniac that you see only too often here behind the wheel of a car.

Should you decide to opt for village life, try to ensure that you are picking a good one and not one of the *malsain* (unhealthy) sick ones that unfortunately do exist. Talk to people in the vicinity. Drive slowly through the village. Do people smile at you? Do they seem happy and friendly? Do they stare at you as if you've just rolled off a mothership from the planet Venus?

Q *'Do I want an old house?'*

Probably. Most of us do. It's your own little bit of French *patrimoine*. But do you **really** want one? If you've seen the old Cary Grant film, *Mr. Blandings Builds His Dream Home* (re-made, alas, as *The Money Pit*), let that serve as a salutary lesson. Some of these old houses can be just that: money pits. You could be throwing your hard-earned cash at them for the duration. And, if you've bought it for holiday purposes, do you want to be spending your precious recuperation time doing odd jobs to try and put things right? Many people I know never actually finish, either. You get to a certain point when either your energy flags or your resources run out and you think, 'I can live with it like this for the next few years'. Or you appear to have finished it only to discover that it's time now to go back and review the work you completed six years earlier.

There are many who thrive on DIY, however. Renovation projects can be a challenge, even fun. It's probably worth defining our terms at this point. 'To renovate' actually means to renew. To some, renovation will mean a chance to rip out the old and put in the new, sometimes with quite gay abandon and lack of respect for the property. It's almost like someone who decides to have all his teeth out at the same time and replace them with a nice shiny set of falsies: it just doesn't look right. I'll use the term 'renovation' throughout this book to encompass the rather more specialist art of restoration, sure in the knowledge that we Brits – perhaps because we're so in love with our old houses – tend to renovate them with good taste. Locals might mutter darkly about foreigners buying up their old houses, but they also respect a job well done and recognise that their fellow countrymen (often for reasons of cost) cannot be bothered to do it themselves.

The good news is that renovating a house in France can come with a tax incentive. The bad news is that, as from 1 November 2006, the French government introduced new regulations to clarify (or, some might argue, to complicate) the law. The current standard rate of TVA is 20 per cent. Up until 1 November 2006, artisans (the generic term often used to cover most professionals and tradesmen) were able to invoice labour and materials at a rate of 5.5 per cent if the customer declared on an *attestation* that the property to be renovated was more than two years old. The government then determined that TVA would stay at 5.5 per cent until 2012, whereupon the rate was raised to 7% – but only for *certain categories* of renovation. At the danger of being too simplistic, if it's a matter of employing *registered* professionals to maintain, refurbish or generally improve (without significantly increasing the surface area of) a property that was previously lived in, the rate – for certain materials and most but not all aspects of the work – is currently 7 per cent. However, conversions of roof spaces and agricultural barns (that were not previously lived in and thus become effectively new 'lodgings') are rated at 19.6 per cent. So it could add 14 per cent to your budget.

Like everything here, though, the stipulations are open to a certain degree of interpretation, so there can be the confusing situation of paying different rates of TVA for different parts of the renovation. Moreover, the new *attestation* to be completed and signed by the owner of the property in order to claim the preferential rate of TVA is more precise and therefore more complicated and more stringent (although one of the two new models used is ironically called an *attestation simplifiée*). Since the artisan could be made liable for any additional tax if a government inspector finds that a particular aspect of the work should have been invoiced at 19.6 per cent, that artisan will no doubt be more wary of accepting at face value *attestations* from customers.

Other fiscal incentives (for income tax payers in France) – towards greener heating solutions, for example – and grants exist, although they are constantly subject to modifications as penny-pinching politicians renege on their promises. The latter vary from area to area according to local heritage initiatives. You can obtain details from the local *mairie*, but it's worth noting that they always come with strings attached, such as having to keep the house for a certain number of years before selling. Another source of useful information on such matters is ADIL (Agence Départementale pour l'Information sur le Logement) – part of a national non-profit-making organisation (ANIL), dispensing free information on most housing matters to the general public. Their website – www.anil.org – has some useful information translated into English and will also provide the contact details for the nearest ADIL agency.

Q *'How much renovation work am I prepared to do?'*

An integral part of the decision to buy an old house (one which we'll assume needs some degree of renovation) is an honest appraisal of just how much you're prepared to do. I mean by that both the scale of the renovation and the extent of your own involvement in it – whether doing it all yourself, or managing people to do it for you. Experienced local property renovator, Tim Mannakee, has a golden rule of renovation: 'It will take twice as long and cost twice as much as you think. Don't kid yourself into thinking that it won't; it will.' Are you prepared to go the distance, or will you be satisfied with some compromises and half-measures?

Just to give you an idea of what's really involved in doing it all yourself, there was a little stone house, not much bigger than a Wendy house, on the edge of our former village. One of the old *'mamies'* (old ladies) would use the patch of garden in front to grow vegetables. The house looked without hope: it was falling to bits and a massive wisteria grew out of the sole chimney, flowering spectacularly and incongruously once every year – as if someone were burning goober-dust within. Then a mild-mannered man who presumably owned the ruin started coming to the village in his white van. He would come every weekday and every weekend and spend as long as the light and the weather permitted. I would often walk past him with our dog and check out his progress. He started by knocking down the edifice. Then he used the pile of stones to re-construct it very methodically and, despite never having been taught, very expertly. He built the roof, using new beams and reclaimed Corrézian slate *ardoises,* each one cleaned and polished by his wife. He built a terrace outside the kitchen and a double garage and the artisans moved in to install the electrics and the partition walls. The whole operation must have taken four years. Virtually every single day from morning till night. We concluded that he had taken his retirement and couldn't bear to spend the time with his wife. Finally, in an amazing selfless gesture, he installed his son and his daughter-in-law. A wedding present, perhaps? It was an incredible labour of love that never ceases to impress me. The French have one word to acknowledge such an effort: *chapeau.* You've got to take your hat off to anyone so dedicated.

Q *'Would I be better off buying a modern house?'*

Quite possibly. Logic suggests that this has to represent the future, because the stock of available traditional houses will steadily diminish. Local estate agent, Jessica Wall, maintains that you get rather more for your money – certainly in terms of energy efficiency, the light factor and the general 'kit', if not, perhaps, character. Added to that, they tend to be a sensible size with a garage and recognisable garden. The wiring and plumbing will be more up to date. Fewer draughts and proper foundations. No wild invasive back-breaking terrain to tend to. Less upkeep and maintenance all round. This could be a perfectly sensible option, particularly if it's a holiday home and you want to spend the limited time available doing what you should do on holiday. Not a bad all-year-round rental prospect either, as tenants tend to value mod cons and comfort over character.

Character, though; there's the rub. Somehow, French modern homes by the sea don't seem quite as bad as their equivalents in the heart of the country, maybe because they smack of Cannes and other exotic places. However, the block-built *pavillons* (as they're termed) that spring up all over the countryside, dotted about among venerable stone houses, just don't seem to belong. They go up in next to no time: within months of the foundations being dug, it seems, there's a uniform two-car, two-child family installed. A few months down the line, the grey concrete *parpaeng* get covered with some saccharine shade of *crepi* (a kind of rough cast render or plaster) and hey presto it's ready for the Christmas lights and climbing Santas.

Unless you've got pots of money, you're unlikely to find a modern house with any real distinctive marks. But my guess is that most British property-hunters in France will not be satisfied with something that lacks individuality. It's easier to put your own stamp on an old stone house, and I think, too, that if you have a rural (as opposed to coastal) *gîte* in mind, you'll find it easier to rent out an old house than a modern one. French holidaymakers won't mind, but they're not generally prepared to pay the kind of money that Brits will. Jessica Wall confirms that most of her British buyers are looking for an old house. Which means, of course, that there is less market pressure on modern properties, thus making them better value for money. But hurry – the gap is closing.

Q. *'Is building a house the best option?'*

If the prospect of renovating an old house scares you and the idea of a modern *pavillon* doesn't press your buttons, then maybe you should consider finding some land and building your own property on it. Though, admittedly, this is easier said than done. We were incredibly fortunate to find our plot with a view and had checked out some pretty uninspiring sites before we were presented with an opportunity not to be missed.

Unsurprisingly I suppose, the search for suitable land has become more difficult in recent years. For one thing, there's only a finite amount available even in a big country like France – and it's important to remember that in days gone by people built their houses when they had the pick of the land. There were few if any planning laws at the time and they chose to build where they did for a reason (which suggests that they rejected other potential sites for an equally good reason). So the current dwindling stock of available land constitutes, by and large, the land that was sniffed at by the choosy builders of yore.

Planning laws have become more onerous. Technically, you can only build on a plot of land if it comes with a C.U. – a *certificat d'urbanisme*. In simplistic terms, a C.U. is outline planning permission: a kind of guarantee that you can at least have the basic essential services (such as water and electricity). The governing body, the DDE (*Direction Départmentale de l'Equipement*), will now only issue a C.U. if the land is near existing essential-services supplies. Which means that the dream plot, the one with the magnificent view and the healthy distance from any neighbours, is increasingly becoming a mirage. If you do manage to find something suitable, the asking price will almost certainly be lower than its UK equivalent, but no longer a snip.

If the search for virgin land proves fruitless, another way of going about the business of building something modern is to find something old. The prospect of restoring a ruin might seem daunting until you consider that effectively what you're doing is just building a new house using up to four available walls. And if you don't wish to be constrained by the existing outline, you can always knock it down and start from scratch (provided that you seek the necessary permission). For one thing, there'll be a pile of otherwise expensive stones to use. Although you'll still need the initial C.U., it shouldn't prove too difficult if the land already accommodated a building (although regulations vary from region to region).

As for cost, I've already suggested that, compared to a full-blown renovation, it can actually be cheaper to start from scratch. What's more, building your own home means that your plans are not dictated by any existing shapes (even the rudimentary rectangle of an agricultural barn can be limiting) and you can choose everything from the layout of the rooms to the siting of electrical sockets. It could be a once-in-a-lifetime opportunity to create your perfect living environment.

On the subject of environment, Paul and Jill Foulkes decided to build a house that could serve as a model for other self-builders interested in creating a home with minimal environmental impact. Apart from the obvious play on the prefix 'eco', they called it the Echo House, because the idea is that others can use the template to create their own version of a comfortable modern home that is both cheap to build and (very) cheap to run. You can find out more via their website, www.echohouse.eu.

Q. *'What about a kit-house?'*

Building your own home still presents the problem of finding the time to do it yourself or, at the very least, project-manage it all yourself. One viable variation on a theme – particularly if your time in France is at a premium – is to put it all in the hands of others. In most sizeable towns here, you'll see at least one shop window displaying houses that appear a little unreal. These are the purveyors of *pavillons de parpaing*. You can go in, flick through a book of samples, choose the one you like the look of and the company will (for a price of course, though one that needn't be exorbitant) handle everything from plans and permissions to plumbing and plastering.

The range of designs available may be limited, but there are ever more providers in the market. The standard wooden house, for example, may be a fairly basic beast, but these days there are many more raw materials to choose from: whole logs, interlocking panels of wood chip, softwood from France, Sweden, Russia, Poland, hardwood from Canada and Brazil and anywhere else prepared to ship its dwindling supply of natural resources to Western Europe. There are those who find them offensive because they don't seem to fit in with the traditional indigenous property, but – if done with taste and a certain distinction – they offend much less than the unimaginative copies and crass imitations that are the architectural version of mutton dressed up as lamb.

Prices of off-the-peg wooden houses are reasonable and it's amazing how quickly they can go up. Near us, for example, a concrete pad was poured on a tiny plot at the edge of a traditional (and rather depressing) farming village. As soon as the white vans turned up, within a week a seemingly finished house sat on the pad. But beware. An acquaintance of mine has a similarly erected wooden house in the valley below. To all intents and purpose, it has been finished for two years. However, he's still waiting for the plumber to come and finish the sanitary fittings. Whatever the service offered, the customer still needs to ensure that things are done as promised.

And – if you're thinking of a wooden kit – please remember to check your sources carefully. While the Russian deal seems cheaper than the Swedish package, consider the long-term cost of using wood from a forest that's not properly managed.

Remember, too, that the quality of the finished kit house will vary as much as the price. If you choose something that's cheaper because, for instance, it uses inferior materials, when it comes to selling it, this compromise will be reflected in the price you obtain.

Q. 'Would an apartment rather than a house better suit my needs?'

Yes, it's a true – this is a book about buying a **house** in France. Nevertheless, there are plenty of apartments on the market and perhaps this option would suit you better. However… you won't be unduly surprised to discover that there are certain peculiarities and pitfalls to negotiate.

Unlike the UK, where most flats are sold leasehold, all apartments in France are sold freehold. Let's take the not uncommon example of a converted chateau. Each proprietor of his or her particular converted apartment is also a *copropriétaire* of the chateau in which it is situated. All the *copropriétaires* belong to a syndicate (*syndicat de copropriété*), which is responsible for the upkeep of the building and its common areas (such as the grounds, the swimming pool and so forth). So, when you go looking at your potential apartment, you need to think about the potential annual expense that this will involve.

The *syndicat* meets annually at an *assemblée générale* to vote on all the issues relevant to running the place for the next year. This will include setting the budget for necessary repairs and other anticipated expenditure. It is the individual appointed to manage the building who convenes the annual meeting. This individual could be a professional (a *syndic professionel*) or one of the *copropriétaires* happy to take on the role (a *syndic non professionel*) and covered, it is recommended though not obligatory, by third party insurance. There should also be an elected *conseil syndical* (an advisory body of *copropriétaires*) to assist and oversee the syndic in the running of the *syndicat*, and an elected *président* to oversee and lead the *assemblée générale* and liaise between the syndic and the *copropriétaires*.

Having read this last paragraph, you might appreciate why French meetings can be possibly the most tedious affairs on earth. Everyone talks and talks and talks until, worn out by the intensity of the frenetic dialogue, they take a vote on the matter and then, because certain people continue to talk and talk and talk with ever more fervour, the democratically agreed decision is overturned by those who make the most noise. If you buy into a French-owned *syndicat*, take a good book and/or an MP3 player to meetings and don't take it personally if your vote is overridden by the most voluble *copropriétaires*.

The 'weight' of your vote, incidentally, corresponds to the value of your *tantième*: a kind of percentage of ownership by which each *copropriétaire* can calculate his or her overall share in the property and the proportion of the overall annual charges levied.

Given that your overall happiness might depend on the relationship you have with your fellow *copropriétaires*, it would seem prudent to meet as many of them as possible before you make any decision about the apartment. As you can no doubt divine, the whole area is a potential minefield, and the government has even set up a website devoted to the subject: www.coproprietes.org.

Q. *'Where should I start my search?'*

Let's suppose that you're fairly clear in your mind now as to what you're after. Without having to get on a train or a boat or a plane and come to France, where could you usefully embark upon your preliminary search?

The Internet, of course! I need hardly tell anyone even just a little familiar with the world of IT that you can use a search engine to locate a list of property for sale in Brittany. From here you will be able to locate a number of web-based agencies that hold details of likely property for sale. When we sold our house in the Corrèze, we lodged our details on one of these sites. Our eventual buyer phoned us up one evening at dinner time. My wife (in her usual rash, ingenuous fashion) suggested that she come and stay with us for a couple of nights so she could experience the local life. She arrived with her husband, fell in love with the house and bought it.

You can use the Internet to locate UK-based estate agents that specialise in French property, or try checking out the small ads in one of several publications to be found on a newsagent's shelves. I've written for *France Magazine* and *French Property News*, so naturally must flag them up. The good thing about these UK-based agencies is that they may let you have more information than some of their reticent French colleagues. (The prevalent culture is to withhold the key facts until you've seen the place, which has always struck me as topsy-turvy.) And don't worry that you will have to pay two sets of agency fees: the UK agency will take a cut of the French agency's fees.

It may, however, be quicker and more efficient to go direct to a French agency (particularly as more and more now provide an English-speaking service). Jessica Wall has plenty of clients who will contact her initially direct from the UK – usually by e-mail. She's happy to answer enquiries either by e-mail or telephone. For reasons of speed and price, she prefers to send details electronically and suggests that if a client doesn't have a computer, there is the option of going to the local library and setting up an e-mail address with one of the free providers (such as Yahoo or Hotmail). You may start off in contact with several agencies and agents, then narrow it down to an individual agency or one particular agent with whom you feel most comfortable. This isn't a bad thing: bearing in mind that this agent will be looking out for details of ideal properties to send you, showing you around some of these properties, negotiating with the vendors on your behalf, accompanying you during the stages of the contractual process and generally advising you throughout, it's as well to work with someone you like and trust. Whomever you put your faith in, just make sure that they have a *carte professionelle* (official license). It means, for one thing, that the agent will be covered by indemnity insurance.

There are, too, an increasing number of British ex-pats who will undertake a personal property search for their clients. They are not professional estate agents, so they won't have a *carte professionelle*, but that's not to say that they can't play an important role in helping you find your ideal property. Friends of mine offer this service from time to time – often for clients who have stayed in one of their *gîtes*. Generally these brokers will facilitate your quest by preparing property portfolios, advising on travel, showing you around the area and so forth. The main benefit to you is that they know the area well and know what it's like to have been in your shoes. Most of them will have a website and some of them will advertise in the kinds of publications I've already mentioned.

If you're very independent and adventurous, you could cut out the middle man altogether and find your property by asking around (at the *mairie*, for example) or by enquiring at *notaires'* offices, since these revered individuals often hold details of some (but not necessarily many) houses for sale in their area. (Very) roughly speaking, *notaires* are the equivalent of solicitors in so far as their job is mainly to do with the composition of legal documents. But they are not employees of some legal firm, they are employed by the state – which, I guess, makes them dreaded *fonctionnaires* (civil servants).

Whichever route you decide to take, the next step obviously is to go out there and get active.

Q. *'Should I consider buying by auction?'*

Buying via a *vente aux enchères publiques* is certainly the fastest and possibly the cheapest way of tracking down property in France. The fastest because there's no conveyancing to go through and you can in theory take possession of your new property 11 days after the auction. The cheapest because it's neither the best known route nor something for your average faint-hearted buyer, and you are therefore more likely to pick up a real bargain. I recently heard, for example, that a rather grand apartment in a château sold at auction for less than half of its previous asking price.

But you need to have your wits about you and you need to be well prepared to act fast. Even after I became aware of the auction route, I never spotted them openly advertised. They are, in fact, advertised in the principal local and regional newspapers in the property classifieds section. The ad should describe the property and tell you the reserve fixed price, where it's located and when you can view it. It will also provide contact details of the *notaire* in charge of the sale. There are three ways in which property might be auctioned: via *notaires* (mainly quick private sales and 'unusual' properties); via *tribunals de grande instance* (county court – mainly mortgage repossessions); and via the State (public buildings and unclaimed property that has, by default, come into the public domain). This last channel was presumably the one used to sell (for a song) all the old SNCF stations that have now been converted mainly into dinky little private homes.

The property itself will display a sign and, although there is no conveyancing involved, a detailed *cahier des charges* specifying all the type of information that a *notaire* would normally spell out in a contract is available for inspection a few weeks before the auction itself.

You should arrange to view the property on one of the dates indicated. Along with the *cahier*, this constitutes all the information you will have at your disposal. So if the property really interests you, ensure that you have sorted out all the financial arrangements so that you are in a position to buy the house if your bid is accepted. In addition to the purchase price, you will be expected to pay the customary taxes for transferring the property as well as a 1 per cent contribution towards the costs of the auction. There will be no special contractual clauses to protect you in the event of failing to secure the necessary finance.

On the day of the auction, you will need to write out a deposit cheque (supported by proof of identity) for at least 20 per cent of the value of the property in question. This entitles you to enter the arena and make official bids (actually by raising a hand – rather than winking or scratching your nose). It is returned in full – without any charges – if your bid is unsuccessful, but it is also forfeited (in full) if you are unable to come up with the rest of the money due in the stipulated time (45 days in the case of a *notaire's* auction or three months if a tribunal's). There is no 'cooling-off' period, but during the ten days following the auction, your winning bid can be – in a sense – gazumped by another offer that is at least 10 per cent of your bid. This in turn necessitates a fresh (though final) auction. But if there is no *surenchère* (higher bid), you will receive a certificate to declare that you are the new owner of the property.

Q. 'When is the best time of year to go looking?'

The temptation is to tie it in with your summer holiday. The drawback is that you probably see something you really like when the sky is blue, the sun is shining and the property looks its best. Unless you know the area well and/or you've got a vivid imagination, you don't get a feel for the house when it's stripped of its make-up and glad rags.

Although her rule of thumb is that you should check out an area at the time of year when you will generally want to be there, Jessica Wall advises clients to try to avoid the peak holiday stampedes. I feel that, even if you're buying with summer lets in mind and you're not planning to live there yourself, it's desirable to view a property off-season. You can assess things like (lack of) exposure to winter sunshine and drainage of rainwater. So once you've found your house, if you know what's likely to happen in winter and if it's not going to be occupied, you can shut it down, drain it off and 'wrap it up' as you would a swimming pool. We have a couple of good friends, for example, who own one of the most stunning properties I've ever seen over here. It's a water mill at the foot of a steep-sided valley. In the summer, it's a venue for picnics and parties and the kind of place that might have inspired one of Edmund Dulac's fairy paintings. In the winter, the sun never reaches them and it's as cold as Kamchatka. The lavatory cisterns have been known to freeze up for weeks at a time. They live in it all year round, however, and they certainly suffer for their enchanted summers.

The ideal time to go looking is in the late autumn when there are fewer tourists and a good chance of balmy weather, and follow it up with a decider sometime later, when winter has transformed the landscape. Realistically, though, once you've seen your dream house, you'll feel the pressure to sign the initial contract and secure it, so it's important to see this advice as general guidelines only.

Q. *'What should I take with me on location?'*

Your agent or broker will be able to advise you as part of the service. They may even put together your travel itinerary and arrange accommodation. Our rule of thumb after days of making lists and checking and re-checking, is: 'passport, tickets and credit cards. Everything else is a luxury.' Travellers' cheques are useful, but no longer indispensable. The passport and a utilities bill (as proof of address) have a multitude of potential uses and should be sufficient to enable you to open a bank account in France, which (as we shall see in a moment) is essential to the process of buying property. So I would suggest that you take a few copies of these documents. You would also be advised to take with you originals and copies of your birth and marriage certificates, a set of recent passport-size photos, a good map, a guide book, the telephone number of your UK bank, a note book and pen(cil), and a camera, so you can record the key details of each property you look at and thus jog your memory when you get back home.

If you're planning to strike swiftly and need to arrange a loan while in France (which we'll discuss later), you will also need: your contract of work or a letter from your employer outlining the details of your job, status and salary; a recent salary slip and your most recent P60; proof of income over a three-year period if you're self-employed (such as certified balance sheets, profit and loss accounts, personal tax returns and your most recent assessment – though I found that potential providers here were, understandably, totally confused by the Inland Revenue's assessments, so I asked the Revenue to provide me with some simple summaries showing gross income, net taxable income and tax actually paid); if you are retired, your pension statement; some kind of proof of unearned income; most recent statements showing any outstanding credit card debts and other existing loans; the last three months' bank statements; and a direct debit mandate for your French bank account.

And finally... don't forget to cancel the milk and arrange for someone to feed the pet(s).

Q. *'How do I go about opening a bank account?'*

One of the most useful bits of preparation you could do – and something that really you should have done as soon as you decided to undertake this adventure – is to open a French bank account.

A French bank is a different beast to the lesser-spotted British variety. You won't be surprised to discover that they do things differently. For many years, for example, I have railed against the fairly exorbitant charge they make for the privilege of possessing and using a credit card.

For the first few bank visits, it really quite shocked me to see that the staff sat without uniforms of any kind behind desks without screens. As often as not, you shake hands with your teller, indulge in a bit of inconsequential chitter-chatter and then get down to business before the people in the queue behind you start smoking from their ears. At the risk of repatriation, this is my judgement after more than two decades: a French bank is generally less formal and less efficient, and more sociable and more expensive than a British bank.

It's easier these days to open an account here than in days gone by (though it's still largely done person-to-person). The financial services industry is more geared up for foreigners. You don't need to be resident in France to operate the account: you can transfer money into it from your UK account or via an Internet specialist such as www.sterlingexchange.co.uk, you can have a cheque book and card, you can pay your bills in France by standing order, direct statements to your UK address, even arrange a loan, but you can't have an overdraft. Don't be aggrieved: even if you *are* resident, overdraft facilities are not the norm. The banking system here seems to exist quite nicely on a system of trust. Cheque cards are not needed as a guarantee, and a shop may or may not ask for proof of identity before they will take a cheque for goods. To write a cheque that will take you into the red without prior authorisation is really frowned upon. Technically speaking, it's illegal to write out a cheque with insufficient funds in your account to cover it. At best, you will be ticked off, at worst you could be fined and even blacklisted.

It's probably best to open a savings account in conjunction with your current account. Admittedly, it will pay a paltry amount of interest, but at least you can hold sufficient funds in this type of account rather than your current account, which pays nothing at all. You can then arrange periodic *virements* (transfers) – by phone or by Internet – to ensure that your main account is topped up to cover the necessary outgoings.

Avoid, however, the temptation to open accounts with more than one bank. Not only will you find each one unnecessarily expensive (French banks are adept at scaring their customers into buying insurance for God-knows-what eventuality), but when the time comes to closing one such surplus account, you might be subjected to some punitive and humiliating sanctions. Let me pass on the benefit of my experience here. A few years ago, I attended an interview at my bank in Tulle (whose name shall be withheld to protect the guilty). The interview was conducted by a fast-talking floozy with false eyelashes in a room kitted out, I realise now, for mass indoctrination. I can assure you that I was not seduced by *Madamoiselle X*'s unsubtle charms. No, it was more the promise of a Visa card and a raft of insurance cover with no charge – but only for a finite period. Needless to say, I managed to let the anniversary date pass and thus found some exorbitant charge itemised on a future statement. As a kind of act of self-flagellation, I paid up without undue protest, but noted in my diary a date several months ahead of the next anniversary.

When I returned the card and informed the clerk that I wanted to revert to my original form of account, I was whisked off to the manager's office for a thorough grilling. Only when I pointed out that I was a good client of many years standing and not a detainee of the Gestapo did he back off, chastened. So the moral of the story is: don't take out unnecessary insurances and, if you ever want to close an account, don't assume that it's your legitimate right.

Q. *'Where should I stay?'*

If the natural temptation is to stay either with friends or in a nice comfortable hotel, perhaps I could put in a word for the *chambre d'hôte*. Provided that you avoid the kind of chamber of horrors (hosted by a gaudy harridan closely related to Basil Fawlty) in which we once inadvertently lodged a visitor, this option seems to best offer the opportunity to talk to the host (for an insight into daily life) and get out and explore the area. A *gîte* could offer the same opportunity if the owners live somewhere on site. To stay with friends is to risk spending too much time enjoying their company rather than getting out for a good look, and being swept away by their enthusiasm for the French experience. A comfortable hotel tends to be an impersonal affair. No one much to talk to for useful insights and too many facilities to enjoy when you should be out getting your hands dirty. Or, of course, there's that good old perennial standby: a campsite. The municipal variety and the small private *campings à la ferme* tend to be considerably cheaper than the all-singing, all-dancing canvas conurbations that congregate in the more obvious tourist locations.

SUMMARY

There are some stunning old properties for sale in most parts of France. Generally they cost significantly less than their equivalents in the UK do. So the temptation is to act like a child with too much pocket money in a sweet shop. It's all too easy to sign your name to something that's too big and too impractical and that doesn't really meet your needs. Be clear about what you really want.

✔ **Where do I want to live: in the middle of the country or in or near a town?**
✔ **Do I want to live in a village?**
✔ **Do I really want an old house?**
✔ **If so, just how much renovation work am I prepared to do?**
✔ **Would it be better to buy a modern house?**
✔ **Is building a house the best option?**
✔ **Should I consider a kit house?**
✔ **Would an apartment be a better option?**

Once a little clearer about this kind of thing, you should be ready to ask:

✔ **Where should I start my search?**
✔ **What's the best time of year to go looking?**
✔ **What should I take with me on location?**
✔ **How do I go about opening a bank account?**
✔ **Where should I stay?**

Chapter 4. *How do I know if I've found what I'm looking for?*

This is pretty much the crunch chapter. This is the stage at which that epic decision has to be made: 'hit or miss, jury?' Niggling away at the back of your mind are those persistent questions: 'Can I afford to take some time and think about it? If I dilly-dally, will someone else snap it up? Should I say yes right here and now?' Well, if it's any comfort, there's always that 'cooling-off period' (which we'll cover in the contractual process in Chapter 7), so if you do say 'yes' there and then and subsequently discover something untoward, it won't be the end of human life as you know it. In this chapter, you'll find some useful questions to ask – not just of yourself, but of other people involved in the process – which will help you make an educated decision.

First though, a *petite vignette* by way of warning. Beware of something to which I've already alluded: the 'French experience'. Ultimately, what you're buying is a house, not a lifestyle (no matter what an estate agent might try to suggest). When friends bought their first house in France many moons ago, they were taken to view the house via the prettiest, most circuitous route imaginable. The estate agent studiously avoided the direct approach to the house, which was much more practical if rather less picturesque. He stopped the car at one point so they could pick some wild strawberries. He stopped off at a little village en route for coffee and croissants. By the time they arrived at the house, they were hooked. They bought the house. Later, of course, they discovered all the drawbacks with it. Reassuringly, and despite certain problems they encountered during the early years, they are still here, 15 years or so later, enjoying the real 'French experience' – with or without wild strawberries.

Q. *'How structurally sound is the house?'*

We'll look at this in more detail during the next chapter when we assess the price of the property in real terms. At this point, however, you want to be sure that, if you're buying something old, it won't collapse in a few years' time.

A house is sometimes referred to in terms of how 'honest' it is. As champion renovator Tim Mannakee explains, 'It's honest if it hasn't been mucked around with. If it's still basically what it was 300 years ago, then you're usually going to be fine. These old stone houses in France were built to last. If they've stood the test of time up to now, there should be no reason why they're not going to last a few more lifetimes. Look at the condition of the roof and the state of the walls. If there are cracks evident, assess whether the house is shifting or whether there's some other logical reason for it. For example, stone walls were usually built with a double skin separated by a cavity and held together by the beams of the roof. Perhaps someone cut out a beam for some reason. Old houses were often built directly onto the ground without foundations, so you could also try to assess whether it seems to sit solidly on the land. If you are a complete novice and a house has a dodgy roof and some scary cracks, then don't touch it.'

'What structural guarantees exist?'

An old house won't have any structural guarantees. But you might be looking at something more modern. How do you ensure that it's not jerry-built? Guarantees, of course, are only as good as the company that provides them. If, say, a local company installed a swimming pool and that company has subsequently gone down the overflow, then the guarantee is worthless. Most (but not all) artisans here, however, have *décennale* insurance that covers them for ten years in the event of any major problems due to defective workmanship. As you can probably guess, the issue of defective workmanship isn't easy to determine. It's done by tribunal, so it can take some time. The vendor may have taken out his or her own insurance policy (*assurance dommages-ouvrage*), which should cover – swiftly – the cost of any necessary repairs.

Q. *'Is the location right?'*

When we were touring the south west in search of our first property, we stumbled upon a grimy agency in Argentat, a very pretty medieval town on the river Dordogne. By this time, we'd viewed a stack of houses, but hadn't had the necessary vision to see the potential in certain ones that, in retrospect, we would have done well to pursue. Inside this unsavoury looking agency there was a big desk behind which was a tatty mural of some autumn view of the Corrèze at its rustic loveliest. Behind the desk sat a weathered man with a thin moustache. He smoked – and coughed – incessantly, and reminded us both of some Sicilian brigand. He told us that he had just the right house for us and showed us a faded Polaroid picture of a house that looked... OK. (The very fact that the photo was so faded should have rung the alarm bells. How long had it been sitting in his dossier? Why hadn't he sold it already if it was such a great deal?) We should never have agreed to get into his beaten-up Mercedes. But we went and we saw and we ended up buying. Not a thought about location. It seemed a good house, the price was right and it wasn't too far from Argentat, which was just such a pretty town.

I shudder to remember our naivety. 'Location, location, location.' Ignore that golden rule and you can find yourself snookered. It's just as important in France as it is in the UK, if rather harder to assess in a foreign country. On a basic level, you can get a feel for the property's (or plot's) immediate situation. Are the surrounding houses pretty or ugly? Are they lived in, abandoned, used as holiday homes? Are there any surrounding plots of land that might be built on?

Let's also look at some supplementary questions that you can pose to your agent as you travel to this likely property in the back of his or her car – assuming that your agent is not a brigand and can be trusted to give you honest answers.

'How far is it from the nearest town?

A figure in kilometres is all very well, but how long will it take to drive those 20 or so kilometres? If the roads wind like tangled extension cables, it could take a good half hour or more to make the journey. Remember that you may have to make that journey several times a week.

If you are planning to create *chambres d'hôte* and/or a *gîte*, remember that your guests will appreciate a town with a few amenities – a town that accommodates rather more than one horse.

'Is it served by mobile shops?'

It's difficult to come up with an accurate translation for this charming facet of French (rural) life. I once wrote an article for *France Magazine* about the young local baker, who would load up his van most days of the week and visit some of the hamlets and more isolated settlements in the area. I spent a day in his company, marvelling at his dedication and patience and good humour. A kind of Corrézian Postman Pat. He would turn up in our village twice a week, come rain or shine. One year when the snow was particularly deep, he called in his Peugeot 205 – presumably more reliable on such treacherous roads – with a boot full of bread. There was also a butcher, a cheese van, a general store, a frozen goods van and even a clothes van. Clearly, even isolation is relative.

'How far is it from the nearest école primaire/collège/lycée?'

The closest primary school may well be nearer than this town that we've situated 20 kilometres away. You need to find out where the nearest ones are and whether you will be served by *transport scolaire*; the estate agent may not know the answer to this one – you may have to find this out at the local *mairie*. There was once a school at the local *commune* (the lowest level of local government; in rural terms, a grouping of several villages and hamlets), which served our old village. A sign of the times, it had been closed down a few years before because there were no longer enough children in the commune to justify its existence. So we had the choice of two nearby schools for our daughter. Only one, though, was served by the *car* (school minibus). We went to see both schools and, perversely, opted for the school that *wasn't* served – necessitating several round trips a day once the canteen situation became intolerable. It's a source of continuing frustration that many school canteens will not cater for vegetarians and that – because of the national obsession with *microbes* – packed lunches are illegal.

'How far is it from the nearest hospital?'

Don't be too hard on your nearest town if it doesn't have a hospital. Generally, it's only the prefecture or sub-prefecture that provide a local general hospital with a casualty unit. Anything less than two hours away is a bonus. However, your medical insurance should cover the cost of sending an ambulance if necessary to pick you up from home and to take you back after your appointment or once you are restored to health.

'How near is the house to a farm?'

Don't get me started on the subject of farmers. Of course there are many about who are the salt of the earth. The young farmer, for example, who supplied the straw bales for this house is now a personal friend.

However, just as in the cautionary tale of the carpenter and the yokels from the back of beyond, French farmers can be a force to be reckoned with. My advice is to handle with due care and diligence. My composite portrait of the worst French farmer goes like this: someone who lives off the fat of his subsidies; who abides by his own set of (anti-)social rules; who dumps his rubbish in a wood; who uses old tyres to set fire to his rubbish when the pile gets too high; who grows tobacco for the third world and corn for the animals that he incarcerates in concrete sheds; who irrigates his crops night and day with a complete disregard for the water supply; who pollutes the said water supply with the foul-smelling slurry that he spreads on his fields; who acquires at a remarkably preferential rate as much land as he can sniff out to supplement all the land that he has already inherited from farming parents, and then sells for building purposes any old derelict out building or plot of surplus land to some callow foreigner for as much money as he can extract; who keeps a pack of hunting dogs caged up in filthy conditions, and hunts with said dogs on any old day of the week, irrespective of the local regulations.

I'm being a little unfair, but it's a stereotype I've assembled over years of scientific observation. Personal preference apart, assessing proximity to a farm is important for a number of practical reasons. Where there are farm animals, for example, there are flies. Far too many flies for comfort and equanimity. Where there's a farm, there is often noise and smell. Sometimes bad, bad smells. And if you're banking on converting a barn, be sure to check that the *élevage* regulations don't apply: if animals are kept in a building situated 50 metres or less from the barn, you won't get planning permission on health grounds. There is, however, nothing for the moment to stop the farmer building an animal shed within sniffing distance of your beautifully converted barn. So be careful.

Tim, however, has a different perspective to offer about farms. Both the family home and his current renovation project are situated at the end of a cul de sac, which passes by a farm. Proximity to a farm actually comforts him. 'What better; what could be safer? Anyone wanting to burgle the property would have to pass the farm – twice.' In both cases, the farmers are fairly surly individuals who keep themselves to themselves. They might keep a wary eye out for passing strangers, but they won't stop to engage in idle chat about the weather or to waste time on aperitifs. It suits Tim fine.

'How close is the house to a road?'

Burglary is a menace that may well worry you, particularly in respect of a second home which may be vacant for long stretches at a time, and a property next to a road could be a prime target. Even if it's a minor country road, it offers a sneak-thief the opportunity to stop and steal and drive away before anyone nearby notices what's going on. Ideally, you want to be sufficiently far from a road without creating problems of access to and from the house.

We Brits know what heavy traffic means and therefore the thought of buying somewhere near a road might induce panic. Remember that French roads are not generally created in the same image. A country road might be comparatively busy in the day with people driving to and from work in a nearby town, yet come evening it might be almost deserted. What you need to determine, perhaps, is the number of lorries that use the road. And is the house close to a long straight stretch of road where people drive too fast? But proximity to a road may not be reason enough to discount an otherwise promising property. Some close friends, for example, live within yodelling distance of the A20 *autoroute*. To be honest, you'd hardly notice. If it were similarly close to the M6, they may well have gone insane by now.

For all that, our daughter's beloved cat, Harvey, was killed here on a road where maybe twenty cars might pass over the course of 24 hours. You can usually discount the noise factor (unless the road is favoured by lorries), but never the danger.

'How close is the house to a river or lake?'

On one hand, proximity to a river or lake is good for business. If you're running some kind of enterprise that depends on paying guests, you can feature this in your publicity material. Canoeing, kayaking, rafting, swimming, fishing, walking, picnics… all that kind of thing. Without a swimming pool, we made almost daily use during the summer months of a beautiful lake near our former house. During winter, it was an eerily silent and breathtaking venue for early morning walks with the dog. During summer, it became a buzzing social focal point. Bring a picnic and meet at the lake. Nearby water also means that you can install a system of geothermic or geothermal heating (which exploits underground temperatures) that will work effectively and fairly cheaply in conjunction with a heat pump and under-floor heating.

On the other hand, until you've experienced it, you would never believe quite how much morning mist can shroud a valley. We're fortunate to sit above it most days and enjoy the added bonus of a landscape transformed into some fluffy inland sea. Sometimes the mist doesn't disperse till the end of the morning, so it can be surprisingly cold down in the valley.

What with this and the possibility of flooding of low-lying land, it's a case of buyer be wary of water.

'Is it served by a good travel network?'

We might think that we can always rely on the automobile, but it isn't half useful to choose somewhere not too far from a railway station or even, though it pains me to say it, an airport. Not only from your own point of view, but also that of guests (whether paying or invited). This too can potentially become a double-edged sword. A couple of recent arrivals travelled back and forth to one of the many little rural airports in France at least once a week for about six months in the year to fetch and carry inquisitive friends, family and other assorted guests.

As for travel to the nearest town by public transport, I wouldn't count on it. Country buses are maybe even fewer and further between than they are in the UK.

Q. *'Is the terrain suitable for my plans?'*

You also need to assess the suitability of the property in terms of its terrain. If you subscribe to the idea of home as castle, don't be seduced by the idea of owning an accompanying estate. A bit of woodland is always useful if you're intending to use an open fire or a wood-burning stove, but too much land can condemn you to the labours of Sisyphus. Depending on the scale of your plans, you want something not too big but big enough. Tim Mannakee, the property developer based in Curemonte, looks for a minimum of 2500 square metres: 'You'll need it for the septic tank and for a pool, good drainage off the land, parking, a sense of space – all that kind of thing. Ideally, there should be a certain amount of land all around the house' – to avoid the kind of potential run-ins with neighbours that I allude to later this chapter.

Unless the terrain is so special that its suitability is immediately apparent, Tim will consider things like the orientation to ensure that there is enough sun in the winter and not too much in the summer. He'll look at the soil to see whether it's fertile or whether the terrain sits on mere bedrock. He'll consider the elevation: whether it's likely to sit above any winter fog. He'll assess ease of access and, if he's planning to carry out any building work, the possible expense of ensuring that materials can be delivered easily.

'Will it be feasible to install a swimming pool?'

It could be a good idea to put in a pool, especially if you're thinking of letting the property. You could get away without one by the sea, but – as we found out to our cost – it's hard to find tenants for a rural *gîte* without one. So for a modest pool of, say, 8 x 4 meters, you will need anything upwards of around 70 square metres of land. More to the point, you will require access for the kind of heavy machinery needed to build the pool.

The most suitable terrain for a pool is 'soft' land with soft water (because limescale can affect your pool machinery and renders ph balance more problematic). Rocky land is, of course, harder and therefore more expensive to dig out, but certainly not out of the question. Nor is sloping land, which actually demands less excavation because you can easily create a flat terrace using the displaced earth.

'Will I need to install a septic tank that conforms to European standards?'

It's very likely if you're buying in the country. The new stringent EC regulations (which we'll touch on in the next chapter) are so recent that most properties on the market will not have *fosses septiques* that come up to scratch. The requirements – and concomitant costs – will vary according to the size of the household and the nature of the terrain. With the right kind of soil, for example, and a house of, say, two bedrooms you could get away with a fosse of 3,000 litres' capacity and a simple sand filter-bed of roughly 20 square metres. It would have to be very troublesome terrain that wouldn't accommodate one of the various sanitation systems recommended, but if necessary there are ways around it. You could, for example, use a bog-standard tank. It would need to be emptied regularly, which could prove fairly expensive, but it would be acceptable.

'Where does the rainwater drain away?'

You want to try to assess the impact of any heavy rain that might fall. Does it, for example, drain away into the land harmlessly? Or are there any potential trouble spots where it might pool somewhere near the house?

What about water that might flow your way from any of the neighbouring properties? Great for them, but not for you. You don't want anyone's septic tank waste flowing past or even into your property.

'What kind of soil is the land made up of?'

The soil where we've chosen to build our house would represent a challenge even to the most competent gardener. It's virtually pure clay on limestone bedrock. Stick a spade in just about anywhere and you'll hit a lump of rock. It's not, therefore, terrific for gardening and, since the topsoil varies in character between a sticky slop and a rock-hard concrete crust, it's more subject than usual to expansion and contraction – with, therefore, settlement implications for the house that sits on it. Find out about your soil and if necessary have it analysed (you can try enquiring at a local quarry), because the nature of your soil will have a bearing on all kinds of plans – from sanitation to gardens.

'Will I need to create a driveway?'

You might have to – and if so, you want to make sure that you can do it on *your* land. Negotiations with neighbours over land and access can be delicate affairs and, if you're not careful, it can all turn rancid. A couple of families in our old village, who used to be great cronies, have been at war for years over an issue of parking. It has involved lawyers, tribunals, no doubt death threats and general unpleasantness. And all because the lady parked her car where she shouldn't have.

To create a driveway can be an expensive affair and sometimes – if it's for the communal good – the commune will pay. But don't count on it. Laying bitumen costs a fair old whack and most people tend to use stones or *gravier* or *castine* (a kind of white gravel commonly used in France) as a substitute. It's rare that this kind of driveway is done so well that heavy rain doesn't create gullies and channels, which eventually turn it into an assault course for 4x4s.

If you share the access to your land, you need to determine the responsibility for upkeep of the track. Is it yours? Is it your neighbour's? Is it shared between you? How is maintenance generally managed? Is it, for example, an ad hoc as-and-when affair? Or is there a written agreement?

'If it's on a slope, how will that affect my plans?'

A slope, provided that it's not too precipitous, needn't be a reason not to buy. One of the biggest disadvantages is actually the driveway. There's an old ruined cottage at the bottom of our land and there's a rural path leading down to it. Whenever this path gets the slightest bit wet, anything other than a tractor or a jeep gets stuck on the way back up. So the Parisian couple that bought it laid some biggish stones to create a recognisable driveway. It's almost made things worse: even in the summer, tyres slip and refuse to grip and getting back up to the road is a lottery. So choose bitumen: the only lasting solution in tricky cases of tyre slip.

If you're intending to build on the land, then deliveries could be difficult and you need to remember that foundations are likely to be more problematic and therefore more expensive. The slope will also affect the design of the house.

Otherwise, sloping land can be a positive advantage when it comes to views and drainage. It needn't preclude a swimming pool, which can be cut into the slope and look rather classy. Similarly, it lends itself to creative gardening, particularly if you enjoy building stone walls. If the slope's too much for a conventional mower or a tractor mower, then the best way of keeping the grass down might be to borrow or buy some sheep.

'What are the boundaries of the land?'

You need to be quite clear about where your land ends and another proprietor's starts. If not, you could find yourself part of a historical or future dispute. A vendor should clarify the property's boundaries before putting the house on the market, but if there is any uncertainty you should call in the services of a *géometre* (a land surveyor), who will come with a wealth of expensive equipment to justify the substantial fee and stake out the territory. Whether the vendor pays for this or you share the cost is open for negotiation.

The Parisian couple's house below ours comes with such a complicated network of tiny plots of land that I imagine they will be negotiating with this and that landowner over the course of the next decade to try and achieve something reasonably geometric and self-contained.

'Are there any rights of way attached to the land?'

When the Sicilian brigand took us in his butterscotch-colour Mercedes to see our first house, we'd no sooner got out of the car than the squat ruddy-faced man from across the road collared us. 'I have a right to cross your land to get to my walnut trees,' he told us. 'That's fine, that's fine,' we said, naively reassuring him that we wouldn't be linking arms to bar his way. Perhaps this was why the house hadn't sold for so long. The old man no doubt collared all prospective purchasers and thoroughly put them off with his talk of shared access.

When I think back, we were presented with so many good reasons for *not* buying the house that we must have been utterly perverse to push on to the contract stage. Either that or we'd looked at so many houses and were growing desperate. As it happened, though, the right of way issue wasn't a problem. The old man actually crossed our garden and walked down the little muddy brook to his glade of walnut trees maybe three or four times a year at most. I remember one of those times vividly: I was leaning on the balcony, surveying my territory, when he emerged from the brook at a positive gallop. He seemed to be in a terrible state: he was flapping his arms around in front of a face that was as red as borsch, and though I didn't understand what he was on about, the tone of his voice suggested distress. Later, we learned that he had disturbed a wasps' nest while he was rooting around for walnuts, and he had been stung 20 times or more. Some years later, he gave up his right of way in return for our dispensation for his tenants to turn their cars on our half of the courtyard (or something obscure like that, which involved a visit to a white-haired *notaire* in Tulle, whose office, situated at the top of some dark winding stairs, was piled high with legal-looking books: a scene straight out of a Balzac novel).

At least we knew about this right of way up front. It was better than finding out about it for the first time at the *notaire's* office and having to make a snap decision whether or not to proceed with the purchase. Though, needless to say, this is exactly what befell us regarding another right of way issue. Our *notaire* informed us that the little pond in our garden actually belonged to a few select worthies of the commune, who had some ancient right to use the water in the pond to irrigate their fields. They therefore had a right of way down beside our new house to access the contentious pond. It sounds like it could have become a recipe for disasters worthy of *Manon des Sources*. In fact, apart from one or two communal congregations to discuss the quality and level of the water, the right of way was rarely exploited. Nevertheless, ask the question and – if the answer is vague – persist. Yes, the *notaire* should research the issue, but it would be better to know about it before the contractual process begins.

'Is there a possibility of purchasing further land?'

Very often in rural areas there will be – but you may have to be patient. If the vendor is a farmer, then you've got a particularly good chance of being able to pick a *parcelle* or two. However, they're no fools some of these farmers, and if you appear too eager to get hold of the extra land you need, then you may find yourself effectively being held to ransom for it. On the other hand, if you make it a prerequisite of buying the house, then who knows what might be found to facilitate the sale? For example, I heard of someone recently buying a run-down house in the area. The vendor had sold off much of the adjoining land to a local farmer and was selling the house with a narrow strip of land adjacent to two of the walls. However, it transpired that the promised land now somehow actually belonged to the farmers' union. The purchaser told the vendor that he wouldn't buy the house without some accessible land. So the vendor went back to the local farmer to see if he could strike a deal. Agricultural land in the area usually sold for €1.5 per square metre, but the wily farmer held out for €15. The vendor bought back 200 square metres of his original land and passed the total cost onto the purchaser. Since this amounted to only an extra €3,000 on top of a bargain selling price, farmer, vendor and buyer were all happy.

If it's not urgent, but something that would be a bonus, you can try spreading the word (subtly) among the community. It's possible that someone eventually will come out of the woodwork with an offer of a parcel of land that could prove suitable.

Acquiring additional land anywhere near the sea might be quite another matter. Such land is not so readily available and tends to sell at a premium.

So be realistic about the likelihood of finding more. It may be possible, but can never be guaranteed. If it's critical to your plans, sort it out before rather than after the contract is signed.

Q. 'Is there hunting in the vicinity?'

If the property is in the country and outside a village or a hamlet, then there is likely to be hunting nearby. Depending on your views about this largely male passion for blood 'sports', this may or may not be a consideration. Although *la chasse* is governed by rules and regulations, in practice some *chasseurs* will abide by their own rules: shoot anything that moves anywhere on any day of the week. If you're planning to live here with your cats, you must resign yourself to having to incarcerate them at weekends and certain days of the week between the months of September and February. We've already lost Dexter to a sniper and I've heard of numerous others who've been shot either by mistake or quite deliberately. On Sundays, it's a positive war zone and you can feel like a prisoner in your own house. You can put up signs to keep hunters off your land, but they may take no notice and you may be tempting some vindictive reprisal.

Q. 'Is it a soft or hard water area?'

We moved (without giving it much thought) from an area of soft water to an area of the hardest water imaginable. Even if you do take the time to find this out, such knowledge wouldn't, I imagine, stop you buying that seemingly ideal property. But it's something to consider, nonetheless. They say that hard water is better for you; it's certainly not better for your electrical goods. You only have to look at the element of an electric kettle to see how devastating scale can be. At first, we were determined not to have a water softener because of the expense and the possible health implications. Finally, we succumbed because it is just so much more pleasant. A water softener costs money to buy, to install and to maintain, but at least you don't need to worry about changing your washing machine every couple of years.

Soft water, too, can have its problems. It's often the product of granite terrain, which is reputedly radioactive and therefore potentially carcinogenic. Our water in the Corrèze was at the opposite end of the scale to our current water supply: it was very soft but acid enough to eat through rubber joints and give us problems with our water heaters. Since soft water also occurs naturally in sandstone, which is untainted by any health scares, it suggests that – in terms of water quality – this must represent the best buy.

Q. *'How near is it to electricity pylons?'*

You can spot our house here from miles away because it's near a prominent pylon on the landscape. Being a worry-wart, I passed restless nights agonising over the proximity. I looked into the matter and, in the end, I decided that it wasn't near enough to warrant missing the opportunity to buy a very special plot of land. A lot of research has been done about the potential health risks of living too close to electricity pylons. Strong evidence suggests that electric and magnetic fields (EMFs) associated with (among other things) high voltage power lines can represent a significant risk of such serious illnesses as leukaemia (particularly in children). A government-sponsored study carried out by the Oxford Childhood Research Group found that children living within 200 metres of high-voltage power lines were twice as likely to contract childhood leukaemia as children living further than 600 metres from them.

Q. *'Is the house already linked to essential services?'*

If the house is near a pylon, you certainly don't need to worry about the feasibility of bringing electricity to the property if it's not already served. It should also be linked to a water supply and a telephone network. Gas, however, doesn't travel too well, though roughly 75 per cent of the population has access to mains gas in France. In the sticks, you'll almost certainly have to use propane, which is a lot more expensive. (Butane, as we discovered in our caravan, freezes when the temperature drops below a certain point.)

Now surely, you might protest, there can't be many houses on the market without essential services. Not in this day and age. Estate agent Jessica Wall assures me that she still sells houses with no such basic mod cons. Fewer with every passing year, certainly, but they still exist. You only have to drive across the *Plateau de Millevaches* in the deepest Corrèze for conclusive proof.

As already discussed, the accessibility of these principal services is the overriding criterion when it comes to deciding whether a plot of land can be granted a *certificat d'urbanisme* (C.U.).

'*What would I need to do to bring in electricity?*'

We'll look at how you actually arrange for your electricity supply to be switched on in the last chapter. At this point, you want to consider what you would need to do to bring in power if it's not already provided. Your agent should be able to advise you, but they will know for sure at the *mairie* where the nearest power supply is located. In most cases, you will be able to arrange for ERDF (*Électricité Réseau Distribution France*) – the power equivalent of Network Rail – to bring a spur down to provide power for the house. If, for reasons of distance from the main supply or the problematic nature of the terrain, it seems simply not feasible, in all probability you won't be granted a C.U.

So what about the solar option? There are cases – few and far between – of a C.U. being refused, but a *permis de construire* being granted. Near us, for example, a spiteful local mayor turned down a C.U. application for a ruin on some land that he himself had failed to buy (for one reason or another). The applicant was so incensed by this undoubtedly fair and objective decision that he decided, notwithstanding, to apply for a *permis de construire* for his renovation project. He got it. He actually managed to bring in his electricity supply from the other side of the nearby departmental 'frontier', but he could equally have installed solar panels. But note that a lack of conventional power supply raises implications about selling the property at a later date.

'What would I need to do to bring in water?'

Again, they will be able to tell you about the nearest supply at the *mairie*. Either you would need to call the SAUR (the principal water company in France) or one of the smaller private *syndicats* that operate in certain areas. (In the Corrèze, we were served by a thickly bearded man named Marcel, who worked for the local *syndicat*. If you had a problem, you called him up and within half an hour he would be there at the door, cigarette stub stuck to the corner of his mouth and trusty wrench at the ready.) Or you would find the name of someone who will come with his divining rods and find a source of water on your land. You can then get a well dug and become self-sufficient. And because water is a precious resource and metered and therefore expensive, think about capturing rainwater, at the very least for watering your garden.

Q. *'Does the house/land come with the necessary basic planning permission?'*

We'll look at the business of finding an architect and submitting an application for planning permission (*permis de construire*) or making a 'declaration of works' (*déclaration des travaux*) in the final chapter. At this stage of your project, you need to find out whether you have the right to alter or extend the house, or build on the land.

A C.U., remember, is the *sine qua non*. So if you are planning to buy a ruin, say, or some land to build a house on it, you need a C.U. before you can then submit your plans and obtain your authorisation in the form of the *permis de construire*.

If it doesn't come with a C.U., either you shouldn't buy it or you should only buy it on the understanding that a C.U. will be forthcoming. (Your *notaire* will insert this stipulation into the draft contract as a *condition suspensive*.) The application involves the preparation of a complicated dossier, which is submitted first to the local *mairie* and then to the DDE. It takes around two months for the decision to be notified. It's tempting to think that a C.U., once granted, is for life. Unfortunately not; it is only valid for a year (though it can be extended by a further year). If you don't get your application for planning permission in on time, you'll first have to reapply for the C.U.

Just to repeat: if the land or property you want to buy hasn't got a C.U. and there is no likelihood of obtaining one, and you're not too interested in living dangerously, walk on by.

'*Might I have to apply for a change of use?*'

It's possible. When you want to change a building's use – from, for example, an agricultural barn to a house – you need to apply for a *changement de destination* (like a *permis de construire*, a type of official planning permission). Our plans for the house in Brive required permission on these grounds. The house was previously divided into two apartments, whereas Deborah is using the ground floor as a clinic and we are refurbishing the apartment above. To obtain it, we had to comply with fairly stringent fire regulations, suspending all the ceilings in the clinic, for example, and putting up two layers of plasterboard.

Barns are a bit of a grey area. Strictly speaking, most were, of course, used for agricultural purposes – though you could argue in many cases that they haven't been used as such for years. However, a barn conversion also tends to involve new window and/or door openings, so you would need a *permis de construire* anyway – on the grounds that you are changing the appearance of the building. As a general rule of thumb, anything major requires a *permis*; anything of fairly low importance (such as a swimming pool or a small extension) requires only a *déclaration des travaux*.

'Do you foresee any problems if I want to extend the house or convert an out building?'

In most cases, it should be fine – with the necessary permission. Earlier in the chapter, I mentioned the *élevage* regulations that would stop you converting a building situated close to a farm building where animals were housed. We'll assume that this isn't the case; we'll assume, too, that you are buying a house with, for example, three outbuildings (all previously used for agricultural purposes) with a view to creating a *gîte* complex. You can apply 'globally' for your planning permission. Or you can apply for permission for each component as and when you are ready to undertake the project. In deciding which way to go about it, you will need to consider that each application for planning permission will involve architectural fees, and that you will be assessed for *taxe d'habitation* on each building in turn as soon as it becomes habitable.

Q. 'What do I need to know about the neighbours?'

You need to know enough about them to be quietly confident that you could live in this house you've located without problems of *voisinage*. In the UK, disputes with neighbours have to be reported and recorded for the benefit of buyer, but they don't in France. That said, it's probably true to say that it's easier to uphold the regulations governing social nuisance in France. If you encounter a problem with noise, smells, smoke and general antisocial behaviour, you can expect the mayor to intervene on your behalf. Then, the next step is to call the *gendarmes*. Mind you, if the source of the antisocial behaviour derives from one of the mayor's elected body of *délégués*, that's a tricky issue. We discovered that one of our former village *délégués* was burning the plastic off old wire in order to salvage and sell the copper. Since we had little confidence in our match-chewing mayor anyway, we had to deal with it as best we could by appealing to this man's sense of social responsibility. I don't believe he understood the concept.

If, by chance, you discover that there was a dispute between the vendor and a close neighbour, this doesn't necessarily mean that you're asking for trouble. The neighbour might be so delighted to be shot of the vendor that he or she will welcome you with open arms. If, however, the neighbour's just the kind of cantankerous so-and-so who's going to be a misery no matter who moves in next door, well... that must be cause for concern. But, of course, you could stumble upon one of these situations in France, England, Slovenia or just about anywhere.

You just need to employ a little discernment and common sense. You could introduce yourself to people as their likely new neighbour and see how they react. If they band together to perform an All Blacks-style haka, it's probably best to forget the whole idea. If you don't get enough of a feeling one way or the other for your new community, pop into a nearby café or restaurant and mention your intention. Does the waiter freeze and drop your cup of coffee? Or drop the cup of coffee as he flings out his arms to embrace you in welcome?

One of the simplest things to do is to make contact with a reasonably well-established ex-pat in the area and ask him or her for any thoughts about the community into which you are hoping to buy. Bad reputations tend to travel far and fast.

Q. 'What do I need to know about the commune?'

The same kind of thing applies. Rogue communes *do* exist, but this may be due to the character of the mayor – and remember that a mayor has to stand for re-election (and you will be able to vote). Most communes will organise social events throughout the year, so there will be regular opportunities to participate in the life of the place. If, for example, you're prepared to help put tables and chairs out for this or that event at the *Salle Polyvalente*, you're likely to be welcomed with open arms.

Go down to the *mairie* and talk to the mayor and/or the secretary, and get a feel for your likely new commune. Our old commune used to organise annual coach trips to places like EuroDisney, Futuroscope and, one year, some awful theme park in the middle of nowhere. Every Christmas, too, there would be a party with a visit from *Père Noël*, who would hand out very plastic but quite expensive toys to each child in turn. We would have preferred for the money to be spent on communal play facilities or a crèche, or sufficient solar panels to provide us with power, but there are some communes that are more progressive than others.

Q. 'Are there any roads or other proposed developments that will affect the location?'

This is really the sphere of the *notaire*. His or her searches should come up with anything major that could affect the purchase. In the meantime, you could go along to the *mairie* and find out about any impending developments. For example, is the plot of land or the property in a zone constructible? If it's on the outskirts of a town, there might be the possibility of a *lotissement* (a housing development) going up. What is at one time a secluded spot may become surrounded by a supermarket and a new housing development.

SUMMARY

When you look over the house that could just be the right one for you, try not to be overcome by the romantic aspects of your adventure. Scrutinise it with all the care and objectivity that you would a house back home. Ask yourself, your agent or your vendor:

✔ **How structurally sound is the house?**
   (La structure est dans quel état?)
   – What structural guarantees exist?
     (Est-ce qu'il y a des garanties de structure?)
✔ **Is the location right?**
   (Est-ce que l'emplacement est idéal?)
   – How far is it from the nearest town?
     (La ville la plus proche est à combien de kilomètres?)
   – Is it served by mobile shops?
     (Est-ce qu'il y a des commerces ambulants?)
   – How far is it from the nearest *école primaire/collège/lycée*?
     (L' école primaire/collège/lycée le plus proche est à combien de kilomètres?)
   – How far is it from the nearest hospital?
     (l'hôpital le plus proche est à combien de kilomètres?)
   – How near is the house to a farm?
     (À quel distance est la ferme la plus proche?)
   – How close is the house to a road?
     (À quel distance est la route la plus proche?)
   – How close is the house to a river or lake?
     (À quel distance est la rivière ou le lac la plus proche?)
✔ **Is it served by a good travel network?**
   (Est-ce que la localité est bien desservie par un réseau routier/réseau ferroviaire/réseau aérien?)
✔ **Is the terrain suitable for my plans?**
   (Est-ce que le terrain convient à mes projets?)

- Will it be feasible to install a swimming pool?
  (Est-ce que le terrain permet la construction d'une piscine?)
- Will I need to install a septic tank that conforms to European standards?
  (Est-ce qu'il faudra installer une fosse septique conforme aux normes Européennes?)
- Where does the rainwater drain away?
  (L'eau de pluie s'écoule où exactement?)
- What kind of soil is the land made up of?
  (C'est quel type de terre ici?)
- Will I need to create a driveway?
  (Est-ce qu'il faudra créer un chemin d'accès?)
- (If the land is on a slope), how will the slope affect my plans?
  (Est-ce que la pente va être contraignante?)
- Where are the boundaries of the land?
  (Où se trouve les limites du terrain?)

✔ **Are there any rights of way attached to the land?**
(Est-ce qu'il y a des droits de passage liés au terrain?)
- Is there a possibility of purchasing further land?
  (Sera-t-il possible d'acheter plus du terrain?)

✔ **Is there hunting in the vicinity?**
(Est-ce qu'on chasse par ici?)

✔ **Is it a soft or hard water area?**
(L'eau de robinet est-elle douce ou calcaire ici?)

✔ **How near is it to any electricity pylons?**
(Où se trouve le pylône le plus proche?

✔ **Is the house already linked to essential services?**
(La maison est-elle déjà équipée avec l'eau et l'électricité?)
- What would I need to do to bring in electricity?
  (Qu'est-ce qu'il faut faire pour avoir l'électricité?)
- What would I need to do to bring in water?
  (Qu'est-ce qu'il faut faire pour avoir l'eau?)

✔ **Does the house/land come with the necessary basic planning permission?**
(Est-ce que la maison/le terrain a déjà le CU?)

✔ **Might I have to apply for a change of use?**
(Est-ce que j'aurai besoin de demander un changement de destination?)

✔ **Do you foresee any problems if I wanted to extend the house or convert an outbuilding?**
(Vous voyez des problèmes si je veux agrandir la maison ou rénover une dépendance?)

✔ **What do I need to know about the neighbours?**
(Qu'est-ce qu'il faut savoir à propos du voisinage?)

✔ **What do I need to know about the commune?**
(Qu'est-ce qu'il faut savoir à propos de la commune?)

✔ **How can I find out whether there are any roads or other proposed developments that will affect the location?**
(Comment je peux découvrir s'il y aura des routes ou d'autres développements qui pourraient affecter la localité?)

Chapter 5. *How much will the house really cost?*

So we've reached the stage where you've seen a house that really seems to fit the bill. You're pretty sure that you want to go ahead and put in an offer – but can you afford it? Presumably you will have an overall budget for the project that takes account of sale price plus the rough cost (if necessary) of transforming it into the kind of state that you visualise. It's easy enough to be seduced by an apparent bargain, but essential to assess the hidden costs in order to understand exactly what financial commitment you are taking on. Can you do it within the budget you have set yourself?

This chapter poses some further questions – to ask primarily of others – to guide you towards this kind of assessment. I speak once more from experience – if not a bitter man, then certainly a chastened one. You may remember that we came looking initially with £15,000 to spend. It doesn't sound much now, but it seemed like quite enough at the time. We were so focused on that figure that it was a shock to discover that the expense didn't end there. For a start, we had to borrow a further £5,000 to pay the unexpectedly exorbitant fees associated with the sale.

Then there was the cost of putting things right, for which we had also failed to account. Our final choice of house had been largely dictated not, of course, by location (as it should have been), but by the asking price. Did it come within that figure of £15,000? Yes, it did. Bingo. But it didn't take long to discover all the things that were wrong with our snip of the century. The lintels (what were they?) above the rear windows were crumbling and needed to be replaced. This necessitated a *maçon* and his team plus scaffolding. At the same time, he could replace the protruding beam that supported the corner of the not inconsiderable roof. It was shot to pieces. As was the guttering, which leaked like a colander when it rained (and, my, it certainly seemed to rain in the Corrèze!). The *maçon* kindly arranged it for us. Unfortunately, his mate was just

about the most expensive artisan in the area. We got back after one protracted absence to find that the copper pipes spouted like a shower head when you turned the mains on. The vendor had been a *bricoleur* (DIY enthusiast), but alas wasn't up to the usual standard. Well, the neighbours murmured, he was of Italian origin, so what could you expect? In fact, his taste was as poor as his workmanship. The twin orange basins in the bathroom would have to go, along with the water-splash tiles and the marble-effect floor tiles. Pretty soon we were spending all our free time and resources on the place.

Eventually, like the US cavalry, my brother rode here in his white van to rip out the plumbing and start all over again. At the same time, we decided to get rid of the breakfast bar that was built like the Berlin Wall and causing the beams underneath in the *cave* to sag. And the crazy-paving flooring – set in cement poured directly onto chipboard –wasn't doing anyone any favours. We got rid of that too. And so it continued. We reached the inevitable conclusion that we would have done better to buy one of the shells that we had looked at in 1989. At least we wouldn't have had to rip out the old before putting in the new.

Why, you may be tempted to ask, didn't we get a survey carried out? Because, I must say in our defence, we were in a country where they don't go in for surveys. I know now that we could have asked or paid for a local builder to come and check the place out. If you or your agent can't answer some of the more technical questions that follow, you would be well advised to cultivate a relationship with a local builder, ideally one who has ideally undertaken renovation work, and ask him.

Q. 'What is the asking price of the house?'

In the UK, the advertised price is just a guide. If there's competition for the sale, then the advertised price may just be the basis for the kind of unsavoury auction in which we had to participate when buying our Sheffield home in 1987. In

France, the price advertised is the maximum price. The vendor is obliged to sell if an agent obtains the asking price.

Q. *'What's included in the price?'*

These days, it's becoming increasingly common for the agent's fees to be included in the overall sale price. If not, you should allow for roughly 10 per cent of the vendor's asking price. It's a lot of money. We resented paying it to our Sicilian brigand. But a really good agent will earn his or her cut.

As for what the vendor includes in the price, that's for the two parties to agree. Legally speaking, the vendor can take away anything that doesn't affect the appearance or structure of the house. So things attached to walls are a slightly ambiguous area and you can get a situation where the vendor decides to remove all of the bookshelves and kitchen units (along with the light bulbs!). You – and your agent – need to be vigilant about this kind of thing and certain items may need to be listed in the initial contract. You can refuse to complete if you subsequently discover that items have gone missing.

Q. *'How open to negotiation is the owner (and why?)'*

Your agent will usually advise you about this and will, if appropriate, negotiate on your behalf. If you're entering into the purchase without an agent, then the vendor may well be less willing to negotiate, reasoning that if you aren't going to have to pay any supplementary agent's fees, you can damn well afford to pay the asking price. This is no doubt a universal real-estate truth, but vendors will probably be more open to negotiation if you are a cash buyer. If you haven't yet raised the money, then the vendor is likely to demand the full whack. This isn't unreasonable, because he or she would be taking a slight risk in taking the house off the market to sell it to someone who has not yet secured the necessary funds. After all, another buyer could come along and offer something nearer the asking price.

'Should I try to negotiate a cash element?'

Readers with criminal tendencies may already appreciate that negotiations might include an undeclared element of cash under the table. Supposedly, it was or is so common that certain *notaires* will turn a blind eye. Certainly I know of one or two people who have done it and lived to tell the tale. Since the cash is undeclared, it is not subject to either the equivalent of stamp duty or any possible capital gains tax – so both parties can derive the benefit. Paper work is so regulated, however, that it could come back to haunt you. For instance, if you sold the house a few years later, you might find yourself paying more capital gains tax than bargained for – because your declared purchase price (minus the cash element) was significantly lower and your eventual profit margin or capital gain therefore greater. Speaking as Nervous O'Toole, I really don't think it's even worth contemplating.

Q. *'May I see the most recent local tax bills to get an idea of how much I will have to pay?'*

You should certainly find this out before you come to any decision about affordability. Yes, you might be able to meet the sales price, but will you be able to find the money every year to pay for the utilities and local taxes? Ask the vendor to show you the relevant bills. Someone else's water, electricity and gas consumption won't necessarily be the same as yours, but it will give you a good idea.

As for the *taxe d'habitation* and *taxe foncière* (together the equivalent of UK council tax), you can be sure of one thing: they won't be getting any cheaper in subsequent years. The amount charged varies from place to place. Generally, they will be much higher in a town than they will be in the country, because you're paying for more services and amenities. The *taxe foncière* is a tax on the property and its land, while the *taxe d'habitation* is a tax on the occupants of the property. For this reason, if you're buying to let, you will need to pay the former, but the tenants will pay the latter. And since the latter is based partly on the number of occupants, you might actually find yourself paying less than the bill the vendor shows you. However, as soon as you start improving the place, your assessment goes up accordingly.

We were very heartened to learn that our new build here would be exempt (as are rural conversions) from *taxe foncière* for two years. However, we were then faced with a mysterious and substantial bill – payable in two parts – linked to the employment of an architect and the provision nationally of an architectural advisory service. If they don't get you one way, they'll get you another.

Q. *'How much should I allow for the notaire's fees?'*

The *notaire*'s fees (which include, of course, a basket of charges and taxes) are not included in the price. Currently, for sales between €50,000 and €200,000, they amount to a further 7 per cent approximately of the value of the transaction (which may not be the same as the final selling price – where, for example, a specific price, either within or over and above the overall asking price, has been assigned to extras like, say, garden machinery or white kitchen goods). The rate decreases to around 6.5 per cent for those over €200,000.

'How much will the equivalent of stamp duty be?'

The fee doesn't include the *droits d'enregistrement* (the equivalent of our stamp duty). Once the commune, the department and the state have all taken their share of the loot, this duty amounts to roughly another 7.3 per cent. It used to be the case that these *droits* amounted to only 0.6 per cent if the property was less than five years old. Alas, this has gone the way of many fiscal concessions in recent years.

Reading this, if you can spot an opportunity to reduce your liability to fees and duty by artificially inflating the value of individual items that could be assigned a separate specific price, bear in mind that – like cash under the table – this could end up costing you more one day in capital gains tax. We'll look at this vexed issue in more detail during the final chapter.

106

Q. 'What kind of state is the roof in?'

Now some questions to ask about the state of the property itself – in no particular order. We shall, however, start with the roof, as it could involve the biggest expense.

People will often gloss over this. If it looks reasonable enough from ground level, fine. But if you're investing thousands of pounds in a house, you just can't afford to be casual about this. A house has got to have a decent cover. If it hasn't, then you've got to see to it before anything else. Roof repairs don't come cheap, but you should look upon it as a great opportunity to render the place watertight, to put in decent insulation, to under-felt the tiles, all that kind of thing.

May I check the underside of the roof from the roof space?'

So how do you go about checking the real state of the roof? Property developer, Tim Mannakee suggests: 'You've got to go up into the roof space with a good torch. Look at the state of the battens. Are they in reasonable order? Or is the wood twisted and a bit powdery? If the tiles are old clay ones, they should really be replaced every 30 years or so. They tend to get brittle and slide off when they are "frosted". And if you can see any daylight, there's going to be a leak at that place.'

Since I've had more experience with the old slate tiles rather than their clay equivalents, I can add that even if the actual slates look in good nick (and remember that they are hewn from solid rock, so they should in theory last an epoch), check the nails that pin them to the boarding underneath. These are what will wear out.

Remember, too, that it's easy to overreact to certain old roofs. Many a prospective buyer will be used to the orderly little roof that you find on top of a town house, but not to the undisciplined rambling billowing roof that you might find on top of a barn or a farmhouse. Initial sighting of such a creation can be alarming to say the least. Some friends came to stay with us in our old Corrézian farmhouse once. The male of the couple was a very tidy, somewhat prissy person, who talked a very systematic DIY project. When he emerged from our roof space, his face was a picture of horror. The beams were buckling, they were riddled with worm, the whole caboodle was likely to cave in on itself in a matter of months. The cost of putting it all right could put us in a debtors' prison for the rest of our born days. I phoned our local builder (the one who had already put right our lintels) with a note of panic in my voice. He came over pronto. He climbed up into the roof space and he emerged after ten minutes or so with that clichéd Gallic shrug. What was the problem? Our roof wasn't going anywhere in a hurry.

'How much might it cost to put right any problems with the roof?'

If a bit of not-too-expensive patching will only delay the inevitable, and you do need to re-do the roof completely, how much might 'a fair bit of money' represent? The roof for our current house cost around €10,000. Bear in mind that it's quite a big surface area, but it's also a fairly simple construction, and I did quite a bit of the labouring myself. By Tim's reckoning, you could be looking at anything between €10,000 and €20,000 to get the job done really well.

Q. 'What kind of state are the walls in?'

Given that old stone walls, as I've mentioned, tended to be built in two skins, a certain amount of bowing in the exterior skin should probably not alarm you too much. It can usually be corrected quite easily. With cracks, you need to determine the likely cause and whether they are still moving. They can be tied, unless really serious. Often, though, it's a matter of assessing in an old stone house whether the pointing is serving its purpose. Done properly, good pointing should keep out the rain, but allow the walls to 'breathe'. Which is why you should always use the traditional lime (with perhaps a small percentage of cement for solidity and to speed up the drying process). Re-pointing four stone walls can be a long and wearisome task if you're intending to do it yourself. There are some DIY 're-pointers' I've known who have done a fabulous job; there are others (including, inevitably, myself – and I hang my head with shame) who should have been removed to a place of correction for even contemplating the idea. It will cost more to hire a professional, but they will most probably do it much more quickly, more sensitively and more safely (with scaffolding rather than a ladder).

As for the more modern house, there may be a certain amount of damp penetration to consider. If it's a wooden house, you can quickly gauge whether the protection is in need of renewal. To do this properly, you may well need to remove the old and re-apply three fresh coats of varnish, stain, paint or whatever (even though the temptation is simply to apply a 'fresh lick' of something on top of the old). If it's a block-built *pavillon* of splendour, then the *crépi* may be defective. It may have cracked and blown and therefore let the rainwater in behind. Generically speaking, *crépi* equals a rough cast wall covering; specifically, it is a product popular in France, and (on a small scale) is troweled on from a big tub. The annexe to our farmhouse wore a straitjacket of some *crépi*-like substance that must have been blown on with the force of a jet engine. It successfully covered up the lovely stone underneath with a rock-hard impermeable sheet of something that could only have been removed with jack-hammers.

Q. *'How sound are the timbers?'*

In old stone rural houses, this is fairly self-evident as the timbers are often left exposed as a feature. (This may not be good feng shui, but there hardly seems any point in owning an old house of this genre if you're planning to hide the timbers.) Remember that comforting fact: these places were built to last, so the timbers are likely to be very solid. We'll cover insect attack in just a moment.

Otherwise, you should really only worry if they appear to be bowing unnaturally, or they have been weakened in some way (to accommodate, say, a staircase). In our old house, one of the principal timbers had been eaten away in one section to something that looked very puny. Iron brackets had been used to bridge the gap and connect the sturdy sections on either side. It wasn't pretty, but it seemed to work. And though it's hard work, even load-bearing timbers can be braced or replaced if necessary.

'Could they have been exposed to rainwater for any length of time?'

Tim Mannakee contends that, termites apart, the most damaging agent is water. It's easy enough to see and smell evidence of water damage: discolouration, staining and fungus, for example. It's not quite so easy to spot where a beam joins a wall, which is why he pays the ends particular attention. If the wood has been sitting on damp stone for a long time, with insufficient ventilation, the damage can be quite extensive. In all the time he has been renovating French properties, the only time he has ever seen a beam that was rotten all the way through, it was the extremity that was affected.

'Has the house been treated for insect infestation?'

In this day and age of EC regulations, and depending on the department, the vendor must commission at fairly considerable expense a report on termite activity. (In the Lot, this is obligatory; in the Corrèze, it's only obligatory in the part of the department where termites have been found. Global warming means that the voracious little agents of Hades are ever on the march and it will probably be obligatory everywhere before much longer.) Such a report must be carried out and made available at least three months before completion. Even if termite activity is not found, the report will also include information on woodworm, beetles and other nibblers. If termites *are* found, then the buyer can legally withdraw from the sale. It would certainly provide an opportunity to renegotiate the exact terms of the sale with the vendor, who may or may not engage someone to carry out the necessary work to eradicate the termites and repair the damage. But if the vendor is unwilling to budge, your only option may be to pull out.

If nothing else, this report makes it all rather more scientific and above board, and avoids the kind of situation that I found myself in back in 1989 when we bought our first French house. The house was a network of ancient beams and I could see clear evidence of insect attack. The trouble was, I didn't know the word for woodworm. So I asked the agent about '*termites*'. No no no, of course there weren't any *termites*. I dismissed it as further proof that the man was a rogue and not at all to be trusted. But he wasn't lying. What I should have asked about were *vers du bois* (woodworm).

His answer may not have reassured me. The French have a much more sanguine attitude to attacks on wooden beams. Whereas we Brits tend to throw up our arms in horror at the mere mention of the word 'woodworm', the French tend to argue – very reasonably – that most of these wooden beams you see in old houses are so thick and so strong that even if they are riddled with worm, the heart of the beam is dense enough to resist attack and strong enough to carry on supporting whatever it supports. More worrying are the *capricorns* (the equivalent, I think, of death-watch beetles), which are equipped with big mandibles that can do big damage. They create telltale linear grooves and lozenge-shaped bore holes. However, they tend to concentrate on a few beams rather than attack the whole house in the way that termites do. Nevertheless, it's a disquieting business to lie in bed at night and hear them at work, chomping away on your precious beams. (Finally, we invested our faith in the strength of our chestnut beams and reasoned that, *capricorns* notwithstanding, they would last a few more decades and then some. You can never quite eradicate them totally anyway, and just how many toxic chemicals do you want to go spraying all around your living space?)

The report also protects you from attack from telesales operators, who might otherwise put the fear of God into unsuspecting citizens. 'Our operatives are working in your commune, where we've found considerable evidence of *capricorn* infestation. At no charge to you, Monsieur

Sampson, someone can come at a time convenient to you and carry out a detailed survey...' Friends commissioned some such company to check out the (considerable amount of) wood in their extensive property. To be fair to the company concerned, they didn't recommend extensive treatment. After a thorough survey, they found evidence of *capricorn* attack in only two of the 300-year old beams – which says something very reassuring about the durability of the wood used in the construction of many of these old stone houses.

'Do the professional guarantees cover insect attack?'

Modern houses are likely to come with some kind of guarantee covering this kind of thing. So if a report is commissioned and it *does* find insect activity, the guarantee may well cover this. Because (smaller dimension) softwoods could well have been used in the construction, rather than the traditional, more resistant oak or chestnut, I would tend to be a little less 'philosophical' about the 'minor' insects and either invoke the guarantee or treat the infected areas yourself with a more natural product such as borax (*sel de bor*).

Q. *'What is the energy rating of the house?'*

As a result of EU legislation, houses are now sold – like fridges and other electrical appliances – with an energy rating. Provided that there is some form of heating in the property, the vendor has to commission a DPE (*Diagnostic de Performance Énergetique*) to assess the performance of the house in this respect. This *diagnostic* is likely to be carried out by the same company that carries out surveys for asbestos, lead and insect attack. It won't mean that a colour-coded chart will be posted beside the front door of the house, but you will certainly be able to see the (detailed) results via the agent or *notaire* before you sign anything legally binding.

'How is the house heated?'

Just in case your powers of observation have diminished with time, the energy report will specify this. One of the most romantic aspects of buying an old stone house is the great big open fireplace that often comes with it. Nothing nicer sometimes than to 'cosy-up' by the fireplace and listen to the crackle of logs burning. The estate agent made great play by our impressive *cantou* with its massive stone lintel. In actual fact, the reason they made them so big was that the only way you could keep warm was actually to sit inside the thing, dangerously close to the fire. An open fire, as we discovered in the cold, damp November week when we took possession of our folly, is hopelessly inefficient.

Fortunately, the autumn of 1995 was glorious. We had five weeks of unbroken beautiful weather between the end of September and the beginning of November: just long enough to find someone to install the log-burning stove we bought from the local supermarket. The fire went in easily enough, but fitting the flue (which cost more than the stove and which I had to pick up from a builders' merchant in far-off Ussel in a van that the installer lent me, even though he barely knew me from Adam) was the rough equivalent of trying to push a boa constrictor up a drainpipe.

During our tenancy of the house, we heated ourselves by means of this contraption, which blew hot air into our living space. The hot air rose to the bedrooms immediately above, but the other two bedrooms were often glacial. We hadn't appreciated a) the noise the fan would make, which meant that it was like living with an autogiro, or b) the work involved in keeping it stoked with logs. In hindsight, we should have done our research better. There are many hyper-efficient wood-burning stoves on the market, which produce more heat and use far fewer logs (and even if you're not planning to cut them up yourself, you'll still need to stack and carry them). Not long after buying our house, our buyer realised it was too much work and she found a plumber to put in gas-fired central heating. The house is much warmer, but it cost an arm to install and a leg to run.

Once more, a modern house offers the better deal. For the last decade or so, new houses have been built with energy-efficiency more in mind. There are likely to be double-glazed windows, insulated roofs, floors and walls, and some kind of central heating – perhaps even under-floor heating (which, whether heated by gas or electricity – maybe even produced by the sun or by a heat pump – represents the most comfortable and the most efficient form of central heating on the market). Yes, there are things you can do to make an old house more efficient: you could put more glass into a south-facing wall (for passive solar gain, but extra unwelcome heat in the height of summer) or replace the windows with double-glazed units. However, if you want to preserve the look and character of the original, then both suggestions might be unacceptable.

'How thick is the insulation?'

Again, this will be specified in the report. One of the least expensive and most efficient methods of cutting the cost of heating an old house is, of course, improving the insulation. In days of yore, the occupants of traditional farmhouses would usually store the grain they harvested in the roof space. Trouble with rodents, of course, but a fairly efficient if primitive form of loft insulation. Add to that the custom of lodging the livestock in the *cave*, and you can appreciate that, once there was a good fire going in the fireplace, the house must have been quite snug. (Somewhat smelly, I can imagine, and a tad unhygienic.)

Most houses these days have some kind of insulation: it's a matter of how much and how 'healthy'. The recommended thickness of roof-space insulation is currently around 150mm. There is no regulation to dictate what the insulation is made of. The most common material is *laine de verre* or glass fibre. I've already told you that the roof space in our old farmhouse was enough to give a friend apoplexy. It was insulated after a fashion: with rolls of glass fibre that had lost their initial softness and had started to disintegrate. Every time you climbed up there, you were laying yourself open to future respiratory problems. We should really have taken it all out and started again, but we figured that – like mercury fillings – removal could open a can of worms. We could have laid some new insulation on top of it, but frankly I didn't relish the thought of being too long in that confined space. So we left it and we probably lost a lot of precious heat via that massive roof.

Laine de verre is the most common and most easily obtainable insulation material on the market. Most modern houses will be kitted out with it. Any potential additional expense in this area really depends on your feelings about the material. The manufacturers say it's safe. But if you think about the way contact with it makes you itch, what are those particles doing to the lining of your lungs? The greener alternatives are available (if you look hard enough), but they cost significantly more. Sheep's wool, *chanvre* (hemp), straw bales, recycled paper and such like are all healthy options. We used a combination of duck feathers and sheep's wool (manufactured under the trade name, *Bâtiplume*) rather than hemp mainly because we managed to negotiate a good price.

So while you're checking the underside of the roof, take a look at the state of the insulation and measure its thickness with a ruler. It's not a huge expense, but you'll quickly recoup the investment. You **may** even qualify for a local grant or a tax incentive, although the likelihood seems to diminish as the need for action grows.

'May I see some recent utility bills to get an idea of how much it will cost to run the house?'

As many a vendor might gloss over this with something anodyne like 'Oh it doesn't cost much to heat the house', the only sure way of gauging just *how* much is to look at some recent bills. You'll need to see an electricity bill for a winter quarter or half-year and, if appropriate, ask to see *all* bills for propane gas and oil: it's the number of times that the tank is filled up that's every bit as important as the cost of a re-fill. It's unlikely that the vendor will have any proper bills for wood as local merchants tend to be farmers and others who do it as a sideline, and payment is usually by cash. If the vendor talks about the number of *stères* consumed, the unit is the equivalent of a cubic meter.

Q. 'Do you foresee any problems if I were to change the internal layout?'

Maybe not, if you are converting a barn or renovating a ruin, where you are constrained only by four external walls, a roof and a budget. Modern houses, too, tend to be fairly adaptable, because the internal walls will often be constructed using an aluminium framework and sheets of plasterboard. It's inconvenient to change things around, but not a particularly difficult or costly operation.

One of the great advantages in building your own house is that you can design the layout to suit your needs. Even though your needs change over time, at least you can build your internal walls with half a mind to making relatively painless changes in the future.

However, I've been inside many a dingy farmhouse that cries out for a creative re-make, yet the labyrinth of little rooms, twisting stairs and different levels makes it hard to conceive how to manage it successfully. Some of these old country properties have housed generations of people happy enough to huddle around an open fire while Madame in her floral housecoat rustles up some chunk of animal (previously lodged with its fellow beasts in the *cave* below) on the wood-burning *cuisinière* in a self-contained kitchen kitted out with state-of-the-art Formica. Most of us want something just a little more contemporary. It must be tempting to knock down anything that's not load-bearing, see what you've got and then create something that better pleases the eye of the beholder. But it may be worth the additional expense of getting an architect to come up with, hopefully, an eye-opening concept and some detailed drawings in order to avoid the (alas, not uncommon) situation where a lot of time and effort and a fair bit of money is invested in something that just doesn't quite work.

Q. 'When was the house last re-wired?'

Once again, new houses will have the edge in this respect. Not only will the wiring have been undertaken within living memory, but it will also generally come with some certificate to show that it meets current regulations. While an old town house may well have been re-wired comparatively recently, there are still plenty of old houses in the countryside where you would be lucky to find wire sheathed in plastic. I have seen some Hammer houses of horror in my time, where a careless flick of a light switch could trigger a conflagration. Bear in mind, though, that re-wiring such a death trap could be more time-consuming and therefore expensive than, for instance, installing the electrics from scratch in a barn conversion. First, as the saying goes, you have to get rid of the old.

Initially we thought that the electrics in our first house were pretty damn good. Modern copper wires sheathed in plastic and then fed through grey plastic conduits. Belts and braces. On closer examination, however, we found further examples of our vendor's ineptitude for DIY. It, too, had to go.

If you can cultivate a relationship with a busy electrician in the area who's not too proud, you might be able to save yourself some money by ripping out the old yourself, installing the new wires and conduits and then calling in your spark to wire everything up to the sockets and to the fuse box. Bear in mind that older properties may not be earthed and that a system of radial circuits is used rather than the UK's ring-main system.

Q. 'When was the plumbing put in?'

Partly clouded by our experience of internal irrigation units in the Corrèze and partly because my brother (a plumber) has many times had to put right customers' disgraceful attempts at DIY pipe-work, I would advise you to check this with the owner. If the owner is anything like the old man across the road in our old village, who built his own house and kept absolutely every bill and receipt in orderly files dating back to the Vichy government, he or she should be able to produce the necessary paper work. If not – and you suspect auto-plumbing – try to gauge the quality of general handiwork on show.

The same holds true as for electricity when it comes to newer properties. Whereas you are likely to encounter lead pipes in an old house, which will have to be ripped out and replaced, the plumbing in a new house will be much more up-to-date and safer, and usually covered by some kind of guarantee.

'Does it all function properly?'

Short of flushing every loo and opening every tap, it's obviously rather difficult to gauge whether the pipes perform as they should. Asking the question, however, puts someone on the spot and you can often tell whether someone is blustering or giving you a candid answer. You can also check a bit of exposed pipe for the quality of joints on view and for telltale signs of staining on copper pipes (which generally indicate some kind of leak). It may sound insultingly obvious, but if the pipe work is totally or predominantly PVC, it should be fairly recent and arguably less likely to leak.

Q. *'Do the sanitation arrangements conform to new standards?'*

They probably won't. For one thing, EU regulations change with alarming regularity, while standards become ever more rigorous. Even though we installed a brand new system in 2004 when we built this house, it's probably already behind the times.

There are still properties on the market with no sanitation arrangements at all, and others whose arrangements are primitive. Considering it had been recently installed (presumably by our Italian *bricoleur*), our old *fosse septique* was fairly inexcusable. It had been sunk just outside the back wall of the house, far too close in terms of health and safety considerations, and the soak-away was a hole in the ground filled with stones maybe 15 feet from the exit of the tank. The overflow water was directed towards the soak-away by means of a primitive trench-ette also filled with stones. Sitting outside in the garden was always a bit of a lottery. If someone inside flushed the loo, in a matter of seconds the air was thick with the aroma of domestic sludge. Eventually it 'backed up': either the tank or the pipes or both were so completely blocked, you couldn't flush another thing down. This meant that I had to get out the spade to expose the top (not as difficult as it sounds, because it was sunk far too near the surface) so that the evacuation lorry could get its telescopic proboscis down into the tank and suck out the compacted ordure within. Not nice.

This was luxury, however, compared to the arrangements in the annexe (which had been modernised by the old couple opposite for letting purposes). We discovered that there was no *fosse* and that the effluent went straight into the communal pond in our garden – the same pond that Deborah and I in wellington boots had attempted to unblock with spade and fork during one of our summer 'holidays' (watched quizzically, I might add, by the old man who would have known exactly what we were standing shin-deep in). After discovering the hideous truth, we wrote to the old couple and asked them respectfully to update their sanitary arrangements, since we intended to move over with our baby whom we were reluctant to lose to cholera or typhoid fever. This signalled the start of a bitter septic tank war, which involved tripartite talks at the *mairie* between Deborah, our new next-door neighbour (whose house also bordered the contentious 'pond') and the now widowed old woman. His worship the match-chewing mayor did his ineffectual least to chair the proceedings, and it soon (like most French meetings) disintegrated into chaos despite Deborah's best efforts to conciliate and arbitrate. Although Widow Twanké insisted that there **was** a *fosse septique*, none was ever found when, eventually – and at the gentle behest of the mayor –

she commissioned a man with a mini digger to come and dig a trench and lay a pipe down the communal passage beside our house and then, thanks to our exemplary British reasonableness, across our garden to her piece of land that adjoined our own. Throughout this time, we managed to maintain a position of moral and sanitary superiority by keeping very quiet about our own inadequate arrangements.

Anyway, diplomatic relations were sufficiently restored that the righteous widow was happy, sometime later, to sell the annexe to us (though the selling price most certainly reflected the modernisation of its sanitation). So what happens if you buy a property with inadequate sanitation arrangements? Do you have to factor in the several thousand euros it can cost to install an up-to-the-minute system? Yes and no. Yes, because every home's installation will eventually be inspected. No, because that could be several years down the line, so you probably won't need to sort it out in the immediate future – unless the arrangements are so primitive that you, your neighbours and/or Mother Earth will be in jeopardy. No, too, because there may well be grants available to help with the cost – though this does depend, as it frequently does, on your commune.

The kind of system stipulated by current regulations depends very much on the nature of your terrain. Fortunately, an advisory body has been set up to dispense technical advice to clients. It goes by the somewhat unfortunate acronym of SPANC (*Service/Site de Promotion de l'Assainissement Non Collectif*). There is a very clear and helpful website at www.spanc.fr, which provides diagrams and concise guidance. Essentially, you adapt the type of post-tank filter-bed (*lit filtrant*) system to the characteristics of your land, while respecting certain basic criteria. For a standard two-bedroom home with five principal rooms, you can reckon on a *fosse* with a capacity of 3,000 litres and a filter bed of 20 square metres. For houses with more than five principal rooms, for each extra room the surface area of the filter bed should increase by 5 square metres, while the capacity of the *fosse* should increase by 1,000 litres. There are also a number of requirements about where the components of the system are situated: the filter bed, for example, should be at least 5m from the house, 3m from any bordering land and vegetable beds, and 35m from any well or other water source. We paid around €4,000 for our system – for materials, JCB digger and labour.

But we've already seen that there *are* acceptable alternatives to mains drainage or a suitable *fosse septique*. In the event of insufficient or unsuitable land, a tank would serve provided that you emptied it regularly. We ourselves would have loved to install a reed-bed system, but we feared that, in terms of our *permis de construire*, our straw bale walls would have presented quite enough problems, thank you, without some New Age 'bio-sanitation' nonsense.

Q. 'What state are the outbuildings in?'

A big attraction of buying old rural property in France is that you often get more than just a house. There may also be a barn and even a bread oven. These rural 'conglomerations' are ideal for anyone who plans to go into a *gîte* business. It's tempting to get so carried away with the concept that you focus solely on the main house. You need to assess each convertible property with the same kind of rigour: roof, walls, the works.

'How much might it cost to convert them?'

Some things, of course, like the cost of providing pool, sanitation, proper access and bringing in services only apply once, but the final cost of renovating a whole complex could easily double the actual asking price. I heard of someone who bought a barn for €120,000 and spent a further €280,000 restoring it – to a very high standard, perhaps higher than would suit your purposes, but it shows what kind of figures you *could* be looking at. And because your project will inevitably necessitate an architect, you will have to allow a sizeable fee for drawing up the plans, getting them through the planning process and then, quite possibly, managing the whole project. Remember, too, that every architect and every builder always talks about budgeting for an additional 10 per cent to cover contingencies.

Unless you (or an accompanying friend) are experienced in these matters, it's difficult to know just how much conversion work will cost without engaging a professional to produce an estimate. Builders and artisans are often reluctant to do this before you have signed for a property. Some will do it for a fee on the understanding that the fee will be knocked-off their asking price if you subsequently commission the work.

Q. *'How much might it cost to bring in essential services (if not already provided)?'*

Provision of electricity, gas, water and/or telephone certainly isn't *donné* (gratis), as they say. You would need to contact your nearest agency for each relevant service (well in advance!) to arrange – if necessary – for someone to come and carry out a kind of feasibility study before quoting you a price. All in all, though, the total operation could easily end up costing a couple of thousand euros or more.

'Will it be necessary to bury the power supply underground?'

With electricity, unless you're prepared to pay roughly twice as much to bury the power supply underground, you'll have to accept an overhead cable link from the nearest supply line. Sometimes the commune specifies that you bury the cable, in which case they will probably contribute to the cost. When we bought the land to build our current house, it was part of a *lotissement*, which means that it comes with C.U. and basic services. Electricity, water and telephone were all supplied to points within hailing distance of the eventual house. We then had to bring the services into the house from the various boxes and meters. Services now are generally supplied to the edge of the land nearest a road. Provided that you respect the appropriate regulations, you can save yourself a little money by hiring a digger to excavate a trench to carry all your pipes and cables into the house itself. The individual companies would charge you rather more for this service.

'Are there any grants to install solar panels?'

If you choose the solar option, it is of course a considerable investment, but, as in the UK, you can sell anything generated by your installation that's surplus to your requirements back to the national grid. Because of insufficient winter sun due to our oak wood, we opted for solar-assisted hot water rather than a *Système Solaire Combiné* (for hot water and heating). We installed two small solar panels (about 4 square metres) with the help of a grant (at that time) of around 40 per cent of the cost of materials and installation. They provide almost all our hot water needs between roughly the middle of April and the middle of October. Regulations about grants and tax credits have changed as regularly as the latest Citröen, but you can find out more about financial incentives from the *Agence de l'Environnement et de la Maîtrise de l'Energie* (ADEME) initially via their website www.ademe.fr. It's also worth trying the *Syndicat des Energies Renouvélables* via www.enr.fr.

Q. *'How much should I allow to install a swimming pool?'*

This depends mainly on whether you plan to do it yourself. I'm told that this option is not prohibitively expensive – around €10,000 perhaps – but, personally, I wouldn't know where to start. It would be more feasible, however – with a bit of help – to install an off-the-ground model (which has the benefit of not increasing your *taxe d'habitation* assessment). The cost of something big enough for something approximating 'length-swimming' is around €4-5,000. Where you are planning some kind of *gîte* venture, you will probably want a 'proper' pool that's sunk into the ground. For a fairly modest pool (say, 10m x 4m) that you're not going to install yourself, you will need to budget for something around €20-25,000. Remember, too, that it costs a substantial amount each year just to run a pool (there's the water itself, electricity, water-treatment and so on).

Q. *'How much might it cost to create a proper drive?'*

We've touched previously on the issue of tracks and responsibility for their upkeep. If the responsibility is yours and the track needs converting into something resembling a proper drive, then – depending, of course, on the length of the track – you can get a feel for the potential cost involved if you consider that it costs around €450 per day for the hire of a digger big enough to do the job. The stones themselves, even with delivery charges, are fairly cheap. But, as I've already said, they tend to get washed away in the first torrential downpour, so you would be well advised to put in some of the prefabricated concrete drains that you can buy at most builders merchants.

Q. *'How much of the necessary work am I capable of doing myself?'*

Faced with all this expense, you might persuade yourself that you can do the lion's share yourself. Labour, after all, is always the most costly element. Bearing in mind, though, that this is a foreign country with a particular set of conditions, traditions, materials and techniques, are you really capable? Do you have the necessary experience to carry it through? And would it be a false economy? It could mean taking a considerable time off work. Fine, if you enjoy this kind of thing and you relish the challenge, but might it not be more cost-effective to keep earning the money and paying someone who's no doubt faster, more experienced and more skilled to do the job?

Q. *'How much time have I got at my disposal?'*

If you decide that, yes, you are capable and you will do it yourself, ensure that you allow sufficient time for the project. Remember the maxim: not only will it cost twice as much as you think, it will also take twice as long.

SUMMARY

You've seen the house that is apparently for you. The price seems right; it falls within your pre-ordained budget. But are you being realistic in your assessment of how much it could cost to put it into the kind of state you envisage?

✔ **What is the asking price of the house?**
(Quel est le prix de vente?)
✔ **What is included in the price?**
(Qu'est-ce qui est inclus dans ce prix?)
✔ **How open to negotiations is the owner (and why)?**
(Le propriétaire veut-il bien débattre le prix (et pourquoi)?)
  – Should I try to negotiate a cash element?
    (Est-ce une bonne idée de proposer une partie en liquide?)
✔ **May I see the most recent bills for local taxes to get an idea of how much I will have to pay?**
(Puis-je voir les factures des taxes locales les plus récentes pour avoir une idée de combine il faut payer?)
✔ **How much should I allow for the notaire's fees?**
(Il faut compter sur combien pour les frais du notaire?)
  – How much will the equivalent of stamp duty be?
    (Les frais de droits d'enregistrement seront-ils de combien?)
✔ **What kind of state is the roof in?**
(Le toit est dans quel état?)
  – May I check the underside of the roof from the roof space?
    (Est-ce que je peux monter dans les combles pour voir la toiture?)
✔ **How much might it cost to put right any problems with the roof?**
(Les réparations de la toiture risquent de coûter à peu près combien?)
✔ **What kind of state are the walls in?**
(Les murs sont dans quel état?)

✔ **How sound are the timbers?**
(Les poudres sont-elles solides ou pas?)
  – Could they have been exposed to rainwater for any length of time?
    (Est-ce que les poudres ont été exposées à l'eau de pluie pendant un certain temps?)
  – Has the house been treated for insect infestation?
    (La maison a été traitée contres les insectes?)
  – Do the professional guarantees cover insect attack?
    (Est-ce que les garanties s'appliquent aux infestations des insectes?)

✔ **What is the energy rating of the house?**
(Quel est la catégorie du diagnostic DPE?)
  – How is the house heated?
    (La maison est chauffée comment?)
  – How thick is the insulation?
    (L'isolation est de quelle épaisseur?)
  – May I see some recent utility bills to get an idea of how much it will cost to run the house?
    (Je peux voir des factures récentes pour avoir une idée des frais généraux de la maison?)

✔ **Do you foresee any problems if I were to change the internal layout?**
(Vous voyez des problèmes si on change l'agencement de l'intérieur?)

✔ **When was the house last re-wired?**
(L'électricité a été refaite quand?)

✔ **When was the plumbing put in?**
(La tuyauterie a été refaite quand?)
  – Does it all function properly?
    (Tout fonctionne comme il faut ?)

✔ **Do the sanitation arrangements conform to new standards?**
(Est-ce que les installations sanitaires sont conformes aux nouvelles normes?)

✔ **What state are the outbuildings in?**
(Les dépendances sont dans quel état?)

126

- How much might it cost to convert them?
  (Ca peut coûter à peu près combien pour les aménager?)

✔ **How much might it cost to bring in essential services?**
(Ca peut coûter à peu près combien d'amener les services essentiels?)

- Will it be necessary to bury the power supply underground?
  (Est-ce qu'il faudra enterrer tous les câbles électriques?)

- How could I find out about any grants to install solar panels?
  (Où puis-je me renseigner sur les subventions pour des panneaux solaires?)

✔ **How much should I allow to install a swimming pool?**
(Il faut compter sur combien pour installer une piscine ?)

✔ **How much might it cost to create a proper drive?**
(Ca peut coûter à peu près combien de créer un chemin d'accès correct?)

Chapter 6. *What steps should I take to buy this house?*

Let's remind ourselves where we are in the process. You've now seen the house that you're pretty sure is for you. Your various calculations suggest that you can afford the asking price and all those extras. How do you go about securing it? What are the practical preparatory steps you need to take at this point? Your friendly neighbourhood estate agent should be able to answer most of the following questions.

Q. *'How do I make an offer?'*

If you want the place badly enough and you feel that you could lose it to another prospective buyer, then you should make an offer at this point. If an agent is handling the purchase for you, then obviously let him or her do the negotiating.

You might notice that, in the small ads of local papers, a seller will often not publish an asking price for an item. Instead, you'll see the term: *prix à débattre*. Price to negotiate. Even if your grasp of French is pretty good, numbers are so often confusing. It still consumes precious seconds of concentration to work out exactly what all those figures really mean. So what I'm saying is: if you're planning to do it yourself, rehearse that offer carefully, or you may find the vendor nodding eagerly in response to something well over the asking price. If appropriate, before you voice any offer, ensure that the vendor is aware that it is subject to any of the clauses (such as an offer of the necessary funding) that will eventually be written into the contract.

You can preface the offer with a phrase such as *'je voudrais faire une offre…'*. If the vendor is not impressed, he or she might come back with something like *'Faites un effort'* ('Make an effort', i.e. 'You can do better than that'.)

'What are the legal implications of making an offer?'

If you're scared of committing yourself under the law of a foreign country, don't be. The offer in itself is not legally binding until you sign the contract. Even then, as we'll see in the next chapter, there is a 'cooling-off period' and there are various clauses that will allow you legally to 'walk away' if certain conditions haven't been met. Of course, if you make a habit of making offers on places then withdrawing them for no good reason, your intermediary could grow sufficiently disenchanted to suggest what you can do with your dream of owning French property.

Q. *'What happens next?'*

The great thing about buying property in France is that the process is so transparent. I have never heard of any monkey-business happening once a price has been agreed between buyer and vendor. An Englishman's word is supposedly his bond, yet gazumping seems to be a rather nasty English habit. One of the reasons why it's not part of the French house-buying lexicon is that things seem to proceed remarkably quickly to contract. Just another of those imponderable Gallic paradoxes. In a country where it will take forever and a day to get certain simple things done, you can expect to be sitting down in a matter of days to sign the initial contract (more of which follows in the next chapter).

Q. *'What can I usefully do before signing the initial contract?'*

Potentially, therefore, there may not be a lot of time between your offer and the first part of the contractual procedure. So you should make the most of it! In Chapter 3, we looked at the importance of opening a bank account in preparation for your property venture. So if you haven't done it by now, this would be something vital to do during the hiatus.

Jessica Wall encourages her clients to go back and have a more informal look at the house, and she will accompany them if both parties prefer. So, do things like check on anything that you'd seen that worried you first time round, assess the locality with, perhaps, a more dispassionate eye, and sit down with the agent and the vendor and agree – if you haven't already done so – what's going and what's staying. (Remember that this inventory can be written into the contract.) You could also try out the local facilities. Drink at the bar; eat at the restaurant; ask questions!

Q. *'When is the best time to transfer the money for the purchase?'*

This is a horrible decision for any sentient human being to have to make. Why? Because of the accursed exchange rate. It seems that every major financial transaction we've made in France has coincided with a period of volatility in the currency markets. A sudden dip in the health of sterling can make a considerable difference to the purchase price. Some friends of mine nearby, for example, suffered something like a 20 per cent plunge in the value of sterling between making an offer (and doing their budgetary calculations) and signing the final contract. The money that they had earmarked for home improvements had apparently evaporated. They moved in with just enough spare cash to buy a week's shopping at a local supermarket.

So do you arrange to transfer initially only enough to cover the deposit, or do you transfer the whole purchase price? It's really quite impossible to offer any advice on this. I have, however, discovered that you can order your euros well in advance from certain financial institutions that may offer a preferential exchange rate because they are betting that it will later move in their favour. This I will say: if you're *convinced* that sterling is going to plummet, get the whole amount across without delay. If sterling could go either way, make sure that you take into account the fact that you will be earning maybe 2 per cent less interest over a period of anything up to three or four months while the money languishes in a French bank and you await the call to signatures.

Q. *'What happens if I haven't yet raised the money needed to fund the purchase?'*

I've mentioned that there might be a number of clauses in the contract, which have to be satisfied before the sale can go ahead. There must be a C.U., for example. One of the most common of these *conditions suspensives* – as they are known – relates to the financing of the purchase by loan or mortgage. So while the vendor arranges for the necessary surveys to be carried out (for termites, if appropriate, energy, lead and asbestos) – another *condition suspensive* – you must make the necessary arrangements for the funding of the operation. Technically speaking, you have a month from the signing of the initial contract in which to make these arrangements (though we discovered for ourselves that this is flexible and depends to a considerable extent on the patience of the vendor and the ability of the agent to keep the vendor hanging on). If you fail to raise the necessary finance, the sale cannot go through and you can withdraw without penalty.

Q. *'Will I be able to obtain a UK mortgage for a foreign property?'*

It's in everyone's interests to act quickly. Bearing in mind that it might be easier in the UK to borrow money, should you, therefore, arrange it via a UK financial organisation as opposed to a French one? It *is* possible to obtain a loan or a mortgage to buy an overseas property from certain financial institutions, but it's not the norm and you might spend too much time just identifying a bank or building society that will lend on your new home abroad. Nevertheless, loan finance in France is usually only granted if your earnings are sufficient to cover the monthly repayments, so if you're hoping to use your existing UK house as equity for the necessary funding, this might be the only option.

Q. 'Can I obtain a loan in France to buy the house?'

It's more common and more practical to organise the necessary finance via an establishment in France. If this sounds daunting (and you can probably imagine the amount of paperwork involved), more and more lenders are now offering an English-language service to attract customers. The Credit Agricole now even has a 'Britline'. You will certainly be able to *apply* for a loan or mortgage funding in France (at a rate usually lower than in the UK). Whether or not it will be granted depends, of course, on your circumstances.

'How should I go about it?'

Either you can approach a bank and/or a credit institution (such as the CIF, or *Crédit Immobilier de France*) yourself or via your estate agent, or you can use a broker.

It's advantageous to shop around for the best deal. Having done this myself, I now realise the pitfalls. The banks and other institutions that we approached were very reticent about giving out a straightforward answer without arranging an appointment to see the resident financial expert. The exploratory interview can take up to an hour, as they will want to take down all the relevant details before they can come up with an idea of what it will cost. It's fair enough to an extent, but sometimes you just wish that someone would tell you something simple like '4 per cent fixed over 15 years'. Then, to make a formal application, it seems that you have to open a current account and pretty soon you can find yourself with two or three current accounts on the go (see my words of warning on the subject above). In the end, you might be interested to know, we went with La Banque Postale because they offered the best deal and seemed to be the most efficient of the organisations we approached.

So perhaps you should let a broker find the best deal for you. You can find one in either France or the UK (again, the Internet or a France-oriented magazine would be the best starting point) and even if you have to pay a small fee, it must be worth the advice and practical assistance that they will give you.

Whether or not you do it yourself or via a broker, you will have a fairly intimidating application pack with the requisite form(s) to fill in. You will have to supply information about: you (and your partner, if you are making a joint application); your work and your earned (and unearned) income; any outstanding loans; the property itself; any renovation or general improvement work that you are intending to carry out; your bank account(s). Remind yourself of the various bits of information that you will need to take with you on your property-hunting expeditions (as outlined in Chapter 3). If you are planning to carry out any kind of renovation work on the property, you will also have to provide appropriate artisans' estimates. When speed is of the essence, unless you are very organised this can be a real potential stumbling block.

You can apply for a fixed- (for the entire term) or variable-rate mortgage, depending on whether you feel that lending rates are liable to go up or down. The period for which you can take out the loan depends partly on your employment status. The minimum period is five years and the customary maximum period in France is 15 years, though a 20-year (and even 25-year) repayment schedule is becoming increasingly common.

The government – and the prevalent culture – encourages lenders here to be socially responsible. Excessive debt is to be avoided (so there isn't the kind of level of credit in circulation to which we have become accustomed). Your application will be means-tested and the final decision on how much you can borrow depends on what you can afford to pay back each year (and not on the equity locked into your bricks and mortar back in the UK and not even on the potential rental income that you may derive from the property, though this is taken partly into account). The rule of thumb for a single person is: your total monthly repayments on all outstanding loans should not exceed 30 per cent of your total pre-tax income (this is raised to 33 per cent of combined income for joint applications). Although this varies according to the lender and the nature of the property itself, if your principal residence is in the UK, you will be able to borrow somewhere around 80 per cent maximum of the net price. This figure will be higher if you are buying your main residence and you are already living, working and paying tax in France.

As part of the financial package, you will need to arrange insurance for your life/lives, the property and its contents. Although the life insurance element may necessitate a medical examination, your UK doctor can carry this out.

One last thing – which can come as an unwelcome surprise when you receive your offer (if you haven't considered it up to this point)... The *frais de dossier* or arrangement fee. This is around 1 per cent of the amount of the mortgage. Not inconsiderable. But you should be aware that the lenders will have their own maximum and minimum amounts. If you point out politely that you *could* take your custom to another potential lender, they may apply the minimum rather than the maximum amount. Exceptionally, they may even be prepared to waive the entire *frais*. La Banque Postale don't (or certainly didn't) charge a fee for arranging the mortgage.

'Should I set up an SCI for the purchase and the loan?'

I've mentioned that you can apply for your mortgage or loan on a sole or joint basis. If there are at least two purchasers (normally a husband and wife, who can act as 'shareholders'), you may also wish to consider setting up what amounts to a company for the purpose of buying the property. The regulations governing an SCI (*Société Civile Immobilière*) are, shall we say, fairly recherché. The shareholders own shares in the company rather than the property, which attracts certain fiscal concessions. Most people (French or British) who create an SCI do so as much for a way round the inheritance laws (which we'll look at in the next chapter) as for the associated tax advantages. After much heartache and head-scratching, we finally decided against this route for the house in Brive. Swings, roundabouts and too many complexities to unravel. Your mortgage broker, agent – and certainly the *notaire* – will all be able to advise you about the advantages and disadvantages of this option.

Q. *'Is it advisable to get a survey carried out?'*

You would normally expect a lender to stipulate that you carry out a full survey on the property before any loan is agreed. In France, this isn't the case. The lending institution may carry out a professional valuation, but this is only as an internal risk assessment and it may not even involve an inspection of the property itself.

This is not to stop you arranging a structural survey – and if you lack confidence in your own ability to notice things, then maybe it's prudent – but the French tend not to go in for them. It's part of a pragmatic philosophy that states: if a building has lasted for a hundred years or more, why on earth should it collapse in the next few decades? Modern buildings, as we have seen, are often covered by a raft of guarantees.

'What are the alternatives to a survey?'

Custom and practice here is to take a builder along to check the property (with a view to passing the necessary work his way). If you don't know anyone sufficiently well, you may have to pay for his time. Make sure that you engage someone who knows the area fairly well and who, ideally, has carried out the appropriate type of work that you anticipate.

'How do I go about finding a surveyor?'

Surveyors do exist and your estate agent will probably know of one or more based not a million miles away from the house. Needless to say our rather disreputable agent didn't know of anyone (or he wasn't letting on if he did), so we bought our first house without a formal survey or even an informal once-over from a builder. 13 years later, our buyer engaged a British surveyor based somewhere south of the region. He provided her with a full report that even highlighted the cat flap I had installed in the back door. The report worried her sons, who weren't accustomed to 17th century French farmhouses or the prevalent philosophy, but it didn't stop her buying the house, which still stands firm to this day.

'What kind of legal bearing would a survey report have in France?'

You could certainly use the report (as our buyer did) as a negotiating tool. However, it doesn't have any real legal bearing here, nor is the surveyor legally responsible for anything he or she might have missed. You could try having the survey inserted as one of the *conditions suspensives* in the initial contract, but it's unlikely that it would be accepted. Therefore, if you anticipate pulling out of the purchase as a result of an adverse report, the time to do this would be during the seven-day 'cooling-off' period. And more of this follows in the next chapter.

SUMMARY

You've decided that you can afford the house; this is the one for you. What steps do you need to take now to buy it? Here are some questions to ask of yourself or your estate agent.

✔ **How do I make an offer?**
   (Comment je peux faire une offre ?)
   − What are the legal implications of making an offer?
      (Quels sont les conséquences légales si je fais une offre?)
✔ **What happens next?**
   (Qu'est-ce que se passe ensuit ?)
✔ **What can I usefully do before signing the initial contract?**
   (Qu'est-ce que je peux faire d'utile avant de signer le compromise de vente?)
✔ **When is the best time to transfer the money for the purchase?**
   (Quel est le meilleur moment pour faire le virement du montant d'achat?)
✔ **What happens if I haven't raised the necessary money to fund the purchase?**
   (Qu'est-ce que se passe si je n'ai pas encore obtenu l'argent nécessaire pour l'achat?)
✔ **Will I be able to obtain a UK mortgage for a foreign property?**
   (Me sera-t-il possible d'obtenir un prêt logement au Royaume Uni pour une propriété française?)
✔ **Can I obtain a loan in France to buy the house?**
   (Est-ce que je peux obtenir un emprunt pour acheter la maison auprès d'une banque française?)
   − How should I go about it?
      (Qu'est-ce qu'il faut faire?)
   − Should I set up an SCI for the purchase and the loan?
      (Est-ce une bonne idée de créer une SCI pour l'achat et le prêt?)

✔ **Is it advisable to get a survey carried out?**
(Est-il recommandé d'organiser une expertise?)
  – What are the alternatives to a survey?
    (Quelles sont les autres possibilités à une expertise?)
  – How do I go about finding a surveyor?
    (Comment est-ce que je peux trouver un inspecteur?)
  – What kind of legal bearing would a survey report
    have in France?
    *(Quelle est l'importance légale du rapport d'expertise
    en France?)*

Chapter 7. *What are the stages of the contractual process?*

We come now to the actual purchase of the property. The legal leg, as it were. The conveyancing process may be bewildering, but it's also kind of exciting – like your first visit to a French supermarket. Our first encounter with a *notaire* occurred late one dismal afternoon in mid November 1989, roughly three months after signing our initial contract for the farmhouse. Deborah had battled the appalling weather for over 600 kilometres in a Beetle to get us to the *notaire's* office in Argentat by the appointed time. After spending nearly the whole of those three months back in the UK, I had indulged in a lot of reflection. It seemed by this point that it had all been an act of sheer folly. I took the filthy weather as a bad omen. And I was even prepared to sacrifice our 10 per cent deposit if we could just turn round and go home. Fortunately, my wife was getting used to such neurotic paranoia by then. She was still very positive about the whole venture.

We arrived about five minutes before the appointed rendezvous time and were asked to wait a few minutes in the adjoining *salle d'attente*, where we glimpsed a tall dark stranger who turned out to be the previously unseen vendor. The *notaire*, turned out to be a dark-haired, dark-suited man behind a king-size desk in a dark wood-stained office. So colourless that it was almost film noir. He took us through the final contract, but my French was not good then and I had to rely on my wife for translations and reassurance. Somehow she had managed to convince me that her French was better than I knew, deep down, that it really was. My feeling confirmed the next day in a supermarket when she asked an assistant about inflatable sailors while out hunting for blow-up mattresses!. I signed, as directed, every page of a contract that was quite unintelligible. By this time I was resigned to our fate.

We all stood up and shook hands, and Deborah and I set off for the village with a set of keys and a copy of the unintelligible contract. The agent assured us that he had arranged both electricity and water connection for us. I wasn't confident. By the time we arrived in our village, it was pitch black and pouring with rain once more. We tried all the keys, but none opened the front door. Our fellow villagers all seemed to be shut up for the night behind closed shutters. So we decided to give up and find a hotel for the night. Our little guide to *Logis de France* suggested that there was one in a small town about 20 kilometres away. It was the longest 20 kilometres either of us had ever experienced. Deborah was close to tears with exhaustion. I was numb with the horror of it all. When at last we reached the town, we found the hotel easily enough. It was shut for repairs. So we drove back down to the river valley and along by the teeming Dordogne to Argentat. We found a hotel for the night and slept like dormice. Next morning, we discovered that the hotel was that very day shutting up for the winter.

We went looking for the estate agent to complain about the keys, but found a sign on the agency indicating that he'd taken off for a few days. There was no sign of the *notaire* either. He, too, had apparently taken off for a few days. Definitely a conspiracy. The pair of them were probably splitting our loot with the vendor even as we forlornly trudged that main street.

Eventually we gained access to our house. We broke in as the estate agent had shown us and discovered that one of the keys unlocked the little back door. Eventually I learned to stop worrying about subsidence, renounced my conspiracy theory, learned to drive, settled happily into our house and came to love our adopted country – quirks, dodgy agents, saturnine *notaires* and all.

Fear not. Your own experience will be more transparent with new improved estate agents and the set of essential questions that follows (which you can pose to your estate agent and your *notaire*). And because we are focusing here on French law, you may find it useful to supplement this information by engaging a bilingual independent legal advisor (either in France or in the UK) to help with some of the more obscure technicalities to which you will be signing your name. Or you may prefer to do some research of your own by means of the remarkably transparent and user-friendly government web portal (www.service-public.fr) and/or ADIL (*Agence Départmentale d'Information sur le Logement*), the free housing advisory service for the public.

Q. 'What is the role of the notaire in the contractual process?'

We've had call to use five different *notaires* now; some are better than others, but they're all much of a muchness: pleasant, polite and a teeny bit serious.

An approximation of a solicitor, it certainly seems to be a privileged role. Judging by the fees one pays (though, to be fair, the lion's share goes to… yes, that's right, the state), the salary must be commensurate with the many years of training they go through. Their offices are denoted by a gold symbol, which always reminds me, incongruously, of a pawnbroker's shop. There always seems to be a secretary, unidentified helpers, a waiting room and an inner sanctum.

We've seen that they will sometimes have houses for sale on their books, which suggests that the role is wholly linked to real estate. This isn't the case: it constitutes only approximately half of the role. They also handle other legal matters, including consumer law and town planning. Some, but not all, will be able to help you change the inheritance regime under which any property you own in France will fall. More of that later in this chapter.

Because all documents drafted and signed by a *notaire* are official documents (bearing the seal of the state), the *notaire's* role is crucial to the contractual process. A sale is not a sale until a *notaire* seals it with his or her signature.

Q. 'Which notaire should I use for the purchase?'

The temptation might be to find a *notaire* to represent your interests in the sale of the property. In fact, this isn't really necessary. Technically speaking, *notaires* are impartial – they are, after all, servants of the state, and therefore will ensure that the sale goes through properly so that the state receives its kilo of flesh. However, since you as the buyer will be footing the bill, it's certainly your prerogative to select your own *notaire*. When I think back to our strange meeting with the character from the Balzac novel to exchange rights of way, and when I consider how our neighbour and Maître Vielhomme had probably met while hanging out their muddy washing on the Maginot Line and had been as thick as thieves ever since, I blanch to recall our naivety in those days. To trust that this perfect stranger would represent the best interests of two callow foreigners who would have signed their names to just about anything couched in suitably obscure legal terms...

However, we've always agreed on the appropriate *notaire* with our vendor or buyer and survived to tell the tale. Let your estate agent advise you. He or she will probably have a trusted *notaire* not too far from the office. One *notaire* representing both parties in theory means that there will be fewer complications and that the sale will go through more quickly as a result. If you really can't agree, it is quite acceptable for both parties to appoint their own official, but it's quite unlikely because the total fees would then be divided between you both. What vendor in his or her right mind would voluntarily pay a set of otherwise unnecessary professional fees?

Q. 'What should I do about the inheritance laws at this point?'

Unless you specify to the contrary, your new house will be governed by the French legal regime when it comes to inheritance. While the French law of succession is designed to protect the rights of the children of any partnership, it perversely sows the seeds of much bitter sibling rivalry and general family discord.

Whereas we can leave our property in the UK to anyone we please, in France you can't stipulate in your will that your surviving partner rather than your child(ren) should inherit the house. Technically speaking, the children – as legal inheritors – could evict the surviving partner from his or her former home.

If you came out here to live and anything happened to your partner, you may well be inclined to sell up and go back to the UK. However, if you were left sharing the house with, say, a five-year old child, then you couldn't sell the house till the child reached the age of 17.

'What options do I have?'

So what can you do? The quickest and cheapest option is to ensure that you buy the house *en tontine* as opposed to *en division* – but this is far from ideal. The latter is the common default used these days: it means that you buy the house together and if one partner dies, the surviving partner inherits a 50 per cent share. However, the other 50 per cent share goes to the deceased partner's legal heirs – and this could open up a veritable Pandora's box. *En tontine* means that the survivor will be considered to have owned the property from the start. Therefore, he or she will have the right to live in the property.

No doubt we bought our first house *en division* without a moment's thought and then muttered ineffectually about the importance of sorting it out. Second time around, we specified that we were buying the house under the British matrimonial regime (a *communauté universelle*). This ensures a) that the surviving spouse would be in sole ownership and possession of the house and b) that inheritance tax would not be payable (at least until the surviving spouse's death). Our *notaire* charged us around €300 to do this. Although in theory any *notaire* would have the training to do this for you, it would be best to ask around and find someone who is accustomed to it.

If either of you has children from a previous marriage, this may not be the best option. You can do as our neighbours here did and create an SCI (as we discussed in the previous chapter). Shares in the property company you create are not considered real estate and can therefore be left to whomsoever you choose. Moreover, you can give shares to your children to avoid or temper any future liability to inheritance tax (although any such gifts must be made at least ten years before death).

This is a complicated business and, if unwary, one fraught with potential pitfalls. If in any doubt, you should seek legal advice. Whichever option you ultimately choose, you should also consider making a will, since any will you have made in the UK will not cover your French property. Again, the *notaire* will help you draw one up (for a fairly modest fee). A *testament olographe* is the most common form of will in France. It's written by hand, dated and signed by the 'testator' or 'testatrix' (without the need for a witness). The *notaire* can then register it for you at a central registry (the *fichier de dernier volontés*, as it is poetically known. The file of final wishes...).

It's worth bearing in mind that, since 2007, there is no inheritance tax liability between man and wife in France. Inheritance tax is calculated on the net assets of the deceased and there are quite generous personal allowances in respect of surviving children. The threshold for 2011, for example, was €159,325 for each parent for each child (or for a child for each surviving parent). Liability to inheritance tax depends initially on whether the deceased (and, to a lesser extent, the beneficiary) is considered resident or non-resident in France for tax purposes. If it's the former, then all worldwide assets come within the scope of the French inheritance tax regulations. Needless to say, though, there are complications and equivocations, which make it prudent to seek professional advice.

Q. 'What is the role of the estate agent in the contractual process?'

It's actually a very important role. Normally, you can expect your estate agent to be there with you at every stage. If you speak only a little French, your bilingual agent will really earn his or her fee at this stage by translating and generally overseeing your interests.

As my wife and I discovered during our last purchase, an estate agent is legally entitled to draft the initial contract. Since a *notaire* has always done this for us in the past, it was somewhat confusing. A document drafted by an agent is recognised by law, but it doesn't have the gravitas of a *notaire's* version.

Q. 'What is the initial stage of the contractual process?'

Regardless of who drafts the initial contract, this is the first official stage of the contractual process. I have heard this stage referred to by several names, but it's maybe most helpful to think of it as the *avant-contrat* (or literally 'before-contract'). This preliminary contract is the first of two distinct stages usually separated by at least a couple of months.

In most cases, the actual document you will have to sign is a *compromis de vente* (or *promesse bilatérale*): a kind of bi-party promise of a sale. There is also a *promesse unilatérale de vente*. As the name suggests, this is a one-party promise (although it actually commits both parties to the sale, it's only the purchaser who loses any money if it all goes pear-shaped), but I have never heard of it being used in a transaction.

The *compromis* provides the names and details of the parties involved in the transaction, the agreed selling price and the projected completion date. It lists all the *conditions suspensives* that have to be fulfilled before the sale will go ahead: basic planning permission (the C.U.); absence of termites; proof of ownership; *servitudes* (rights exercised over your property by others, such as the old man's right to cross our land to get to his walnut trees); and *droits de préemption* (the right to purchase the property before anyone else, such as a local farmer's right, under certain circumstances, to buy land that is classified as agricultural); the successful arrangement of an anticipated loan or mortgage; and other less common clauses.

If you are buying an apartment as part of a *copropriété* and you haven't already clarified these points with either the agent or the vendor, then – before you sign the initial contract – you should ask the *notaire* to let you have some important documents and information: the set of rules by which the *copropriété* is run (*le règlement de copropriété*); transcripts of the last three general assemblies; the last provisional budget; the charges paid over the last year; the date when the next funds will be collected.

Q. *'Should I get the preliminary contract translated?'*

Contracts are confusing things at the best of times. Legal language seems designed merely to confuse the very people it ostensibly serves. Even if you come equipped with impeccable French, a *notaire*'s contract is quite daunting. Yes, the *notaire* and your agent will work in tandem to ensure that you grasp the salient points, but you'll want to take it away with you and reflect on its detail during the seven days that follow.

So, if you can find someone who can do it for you quickly and not too expensively, why not get it translated? Perhaps, too, you should think about getting the *notaire* to send you a draft of the final contract (known as the *projet d'acte*) and having that translated so you know what you are signing when the final part of the process occurs. Your agent may know of someone suitable and perhaps even uses his or her services from time to time. Otherwise, it's worth enquiring at the *mairie*; perhaps there's someone within the commune. Alternatively, look in the departmental yellow pages for the telephone number and location of the nearest *Chambre de Commerce et d'Industrie*, which will almost certainly hold details of professional translators.

Out of curiosity and a sense that we really ought to understand what we were signing, we found a local French man who was lodging with a friend of a friend in the same neighbourhood in Sheffield. For a reason that we didn't quite grasp at the time (we put this down to his idiosyncratic English), he was looking for new lodgings and we were looking for a tenant to help pay the bills. One thing led to another and Gaston, as I shall call him, came to live with us. The friend of a friend didn't tell us that she was kicking him out because he had distinct sociopathic tendencies. He helped with the translation of the contract, but it didn't really seem any clearer than it was in French. Moreover, the three months during which he lodged with us were tense (to put it mildly). Eventually we fobbed him off on someone who played the trumpet and lived on the opposite side of the city. We felt that he was better able to cope with Gaston's 'quirky' character. We waved him off with a smile and a big sigh of relief. Both of us felt that we were a little lucky still to be alive.

So if you're thinking of getting your contract(s) translated, just be careful whom you engage to do it.

Q. 'What are my rights as a buyer at this point?'

Once you have signed the *compromis* you should pay a deposit – by cheque, money order, or direct transfer. Normally 10 per cent of the selling price, this deposit effectively secures the purchase. It is held in a special account set up by the agent or the *notaire* and is not cashed until the sale goes through. However, you would forfeit the entire deposit if you pull out of the sale without legitimate reason. If the vendor were to pull out without any legitimate reason, he or she would forfeit an amount that could be as much as double your deposit. In addition, you could sue for any legitimate costs you have incurred – and still legally oblige them to sell.

'Can I pull out of the deal at any point?'

As suggested, not without legitimate reason. So what constitutes 'legitimate'? The sale would not go ahead if any of the *conditions suspensives* were not met, so you could pull out of the deal at the eleventh hour without penalty if this were the case. You also have a seven-day 'cooling off' period following your signature on the *compromis* and, at any time within that period, you can legitimately withdraw from the purchase for any reason. Simply to change your mind and want to go home is fair enough at this stage. However, once that period is up, the *compromis* becomes an *acte définitif.* Once you've reached this point, there's no turning back. Provided that the various *conditions* have been met, you're legally committed to the purchase.

Q. *'What happens in the final stage of the process?'*

The final stage is known as the *acte de vente*, or the final contract or deed of sale. This document is *never* written up by an estate agent; it requires a *notaire*'s seal to legitimise the sale. Between *actes*, the *notaire* will trigger all the necessary searches. He or she will, for example: check that the necessary surveys have been carried out to flag up the presence of lead, asbestos and (if appropriate) termites; investigate the precise nature of any *servitudes* and *droits de préemption*; verify the amount of tax (and duty) you will have to pay on the property and its land; spell out your rights as the new owner; clarify, if appropriate, the issue of basic planning permission; and undertake certain other specific checks in relation to *copropriétés* (shared residencies), new builds (conformity to original plans) and houses less than ten years old ('anti-disaster' insurance). If the property is an apartment in a *copropriété*-owned building more than 15 years old, the results of a *diagnostic technique* (a kind of surveyor's report on the general state of the building) should also be included.

You, too, should do some checking of your own. Before you sign the final contract, visit the property – preferably with your agent – and check that everything is in order. Is it the same house that you agreed to buy? In other words, has the vendor left everything that he or she agreed? Have any agreed repairs been carried out? If not, then the *notaire* may hold back a portion of the selling price to cover repairs or replacements. There is, too, the little matter of payment to arrange. The money should by now be in your French bank account and you will need a banker's draft made out to your *notaire*.

So by now you should be either resigned to your fate or itching to get into that house and start re-fashioning it as you have envisioned. The *notaire* reads through the act, all parties sign each separate sheet of the contract, the financial un-pleasantries are quickly dealt with and you leave with a kind of certificate of ownership and a set of keys (which, hopefully, fit in the appropriate locks).

'*What should I do if I can't be there to sign the final contract?*'

We had only a fleeting glance of our vendor first time round. I guess he must have appointed our shifty agent as his representative with the necessary power of attorney. Normally, both parties attend the final signing – but you will have the option to appoint someone as your representative if, say, you cannot get over from the UK to attend the 'ceremony'. It would be a shame, because it's a generally happy occasion (apart from the realisation that your draft will now be drawn upon).

Q. '*How long does the process take from start to finish?*'

Depending on the diligence of the *notaire* and the complexity of the sale, it tends to take a minimum of three months between the two stages of the contractual process. Why so long? You'll discover that the wheels of *l'administration francais* creak as they describe their relentless circles. So it's reasonable to expect that the whole process from first sight of the house that meets your needs and fulfils your wishes to the final hand-written flourish on the last page of the *acte de vente* will take something like 15 weeks. Much depends on the local DDE, since some of the searches can be potentially lengthy.

Three months isn't long really when you consider that what you've done could dramatically change your life.

SUMMARY

You need to negotiate the various steps of the contractual process before you become the new proprietor of the house. These are questions to ask of yourself, your agent or your *notaire* to help you make sense of it all.

✔ **What is the role of the *notaire* in the contractual process?**
(Quel est le rôle du notaire dans le processus du contrat d'achat?)

✔ **Which *notaire* should I use for the purchase?**
(Quel notaire faut-il utiliser pour cet achat?)

✔ **What should I do about the inheritance laws at this point?**
(Qu'est-ce qu'il faut faire pendant le processus du contrat concernant les lois du succession?)
　– What options do I have?
　(Quelles sont mes options?)

✔ **What is the role of the estate agent in the process?**
(Quel est le rôle de l'agent immobilier dans le processus du contrat de l'achat?)

✔ **What is the initial stage of the contractual process?**
(Quelle est la première étape du processus du contrat de l'achat?)

✔ **Should I get the initial contract translated?**
(Est-ce que c'est une bonne idée de faire traduire le contrat?)

✔ **What are my rights as a buyer at this point?**
(Quels sont mes droits en tant qu'acheteur?)
　– Can I pull out of the deal at any point?
　(Est-ce que je peux me retirer de l'achat à n'importe quell moment?)

✔ **What happens in the final stage of the process?**
(Qu'est-ce qui se passe à la dernière étape de l'achat?)
　– What should I do if I can't be there to sign the final contract?

(Qu'est-ce que je dois faire si je ne peux pas être présent pour signer l'acte de vente?)

✔ **How long does the process take from start to finish?**
(Combien de temps dure le processus entier du contrat de l'achat?)

Chapter 8. *What happens after I've bought the house?*

Now, finally, you own the house. This is the end of the line, or just the beginning of the adventure – depending on which way you want to look at it. You'll have your own plans for the house, but, whatever your intentions, you should find the following questions useful. What are the things that you'll need to do: in the short, medium and longer term? Again, your estate agent and/or your *notaire* should be able to answer all or most of them.

Q. *'What immediate steps should I take?'*

It's quite likely that the first thing you'll want to do when you emerge from the *notaire*'s office is to open a bottle of champagne and celebrate the fact that you now own a house in France. In our case, the most pressing priority was to change the lock so we could use the key-less front door. Needless to say, I fitted the damn thing upside down or the wrong way round, so that you had to turn the key as if to unlock the door in order to lock it. But by this time, I was so bad tempered and frustrated that we decided to live with it. We left a key with the old couple across the road. Every time they used it, no doubt they would shake their heads and reiterate, 'a man who can't do it himself, is no man at all'.

'What checks should I carry out at the property?'

If you neglected to check that everything was as it should have been before you signed the *acte de vente*, then I'm afraid it's too late now if the vendor has gone off with that Art Nouveau *cuisinière* that you had agreed would be staying.

Nevertheless, there are some other useful checks that you could carry out, bearing in mind that winter may be on its way and you don't yet know the house's characteristic weaknesses. Are all the shutters secure, for example? Will they close properly and protect the windows from rain and wind damage? Are the gutters free from leaves and the

152

down-pipes clear of obstructions so all the rain that might fall this winter can flow away harmlessly? Are there any obvious holes in the eaves that could be blocked up to prevent mice, rats, martens, owls and other unwelcome lodgers getting into your roof space? Are there any loose-looking slates or tiles that might slip and allow rainwater into the roof space? Do you know where the main stopcock is located and will it turn off properly? Are the 'hats' on the chimneys secure and therefore unlikely to be blown off in a high wind?

There are probably other checks that the more neurotically challenged might think of. Just be aware that if anything is going to happen to the house, it will usually happen during winter. Be paranoid. Be very paranoid!

'How do I arrange for the electricity to be changed over?'

Hopefully, this will all have been carefully synchronised to happen on the day that you move in. The easiest way to handle the transition is simply to take over the existing contract. This involves someone official coming out to read the meter, so that the vendor pays any outstanding electricity due and you can then start from scratch. EDF (*Electricité de France*) has now been privatised, so be aware that nothing comes free any more. Privatisation has clouded the issue of electrical power. Essentially, ERDF (*Electricité Réseau Distribution France*) is responsible for managing the network that supplies the power and it is ERDF that will connect a new house or conversion to the network. It is an affiliate of EDF, which is the major – but not the only – provider of electricity. Although the two are linked, recent experience suggests that neither knows what the other is up to – or if they do know, they're certainly not telling their customers.

If you can't take over an existing contract, you will have to set up a completely new one, which will involve a trip to your local EDF office (or to your choice of provider) and the customary proof of identity and ownership. At this stage, you should think about whether the supply provided to the house is sufficient for your needs. The system in France is quite different to that in the UK, where the supply is theoretically unlimited and you simply pay for what you use. In France, your *abonnement* (standing order charge) varies according to the number of kilowatts provided, which ranges from 3 to 36kw. So you have to estimate (with the company's guidance) the power supply that will meet your needs and sign a contract accordingly. 6 or 9kw tends to be the norm if you're not heating the whole house with electricity. If you've bought an old farm, then you may also need to change the supply from a thumping *triphasé* to a more modest *monophasé* (which should be quite sufficient for your daily domestic needs).

You might also consider the options available to you: either you pay for your consumption at one level throughout (the '*option base*'), or you opt for a white-meter arrangement (whereby the nocturnal *heures creuses* are charged at a lower rate than the other *heures pleines*).

If you're going to have the house re-wired, you should know that the electricity supplier is not responsible for what happens on your side of the meter. I used to feel fearful and guilty when a blue van stopped at the house and a young man with a clipboard would ask to read our meter. Surely he would uncover the mess that our vendor had made of the re-wiring and condemn our family home… No, once the power has been supplied, it's up to you (and your electrician) what you do with it. However, the suppliers don't want to lose their customers to unnecessary domestic accidents. Before your electricity is connected up in a new or completely renovated property, you will need to obtain a label of conformity provided by an independent organisation (Promotelec) that will arrange for an inspection of your electrical installation. Our vendor wouldn't have got away with it these days.

'How do I arrange for the gas/oil supply to be changed over?'

The natural gas picture is similar to that of electricity. GRDF (*Gaz Réseau Distribution France*) plays a similar role to ERDF in managing the network that supplies natural gas. A number of providers, such as GDF (*Gaz de France*), will supply the gas to your home. Again, you will need to contact the nearest office to arrange to take over an existing contract and get things changed over to your name, or to have the gas switched on. Again, too, there are a number of tariff options according to your likely consumption.

Otherwise, you will need to deal with one of a number of different independent providers of gas supplied via bottle or tank. You can either buy or rent a *citerne* (tank) and you can choose to have it above or buried under the ground. The former option is cheaper, but somewhat unsightly. If you are taking one over from a vendor, it's normal for the purchaser to reimburse the cost of any original deposit. Find out which of the private companies supplies the gas to acquaint them of any such agreements and arrange for a hand-over in the usual way. Since you will be using up whatever's left in the tank, you may need to come up with some kind of compensatory arrangement with the vendor, and then pay the company when it comes to top you up. According to your agreement with the provider, this may occur automatically. I remember once going to check our neighbours' counter and doing a double-take when a tanker pulled up simultaneously. Was it possible that they could read my mind? Are things so sophisticated now? Not so sophisticated that a tank can run dry without vigilance. This is bad news, because air usually gets into the system when the tank is re-filled and the boiler will consequently refuse to reignite.

If you use bottled gas (which is usually quite sufficient for, say, cooking), you can replenish your stocks at a garage or supermarket or even a local shop. You simply take the empty bottle back and it's swapped for a full bottle. The different coloured bottles denote different providers and different gases (butane and propane): there are red ones, blue ones, grey ones and gold ones. Your supplier will probably be one of the Big Four companies (Totalgaz, Primagaz, Butagaz and Antargaz). Should you need, however, to buy a new bottle without bringing back an empty one, you will have to pay a deposit on the bottle as well as its contents. Keep the receipt somewhere safe! It's not a huge amount of money, but it's galling when you come to return the bottle at some future date and the shop or garage refuses to repay your deposit without proof of purchase. There are rules governing the storage of gas bottles (propane for example should be stored outside the house, which is why bottled gas is more commonly butane), and you should remember to check the rubber tube between bottle and implement. There will be a date stamped on it – for a reason. Rubber perishes and may cause a leak. I heard of a restaurant that exploded near our current house (fortunately when empty) and the cause was traced to some old bottles of gas. Connecting a cooker to a gas bottle with a rubber hose is just about the only gas 'installation' that you can carry out yourself without a subsequent inspection – provided, that is, that the hose is no longer than two metres!

For any new installations, the arrangements are similar to those for electricity. Even if you are sufficiently competent to install some or all of the central heating yourself, you would be well advised to use a qualified plumber to connect a gas tank to the house, because standard soft-solder joints will not conform with regulations. Qualigaz is the independent body responsible for inspecting the installation and issuing the necessary certification. You will be astonished to learn that this isn't cheap. To obtain a certificate of conformity costs around the €200 mark. If your work fails to conform, you would have to put it right and then pay for another inspection once you've done so. Nor could you obtain valid house insurance until you have your certificate. A qualified plumber, on the other hand, pays (and therefore invoices) rather less for a certificate, and Qualigaz will only inspect a percentage of professional installations.

Many houses in France have oil-fired central heating. The oil (or *mazout* as it is known) is provided by a wider range of private companies and it can legally be stored in the house. The appropriate arrangements are similar to those for gas supplied via a tank.

'How do I arrange for the water supply to be changed over?'

Much the same applies to domestic water. Taking over an existing contract is the easiest option. It is always metered in France – and rightly so, since it makes customers more aware of how much water they are consuming and effectively offers them a financial incentive to consume less. However, the meter is often located underground for newer installations. Out of sight, out of mind, so remember to check regularly for leaks. The waterman's annual visit once revealed a little split in one of the nuts that connected the meter to our supply pipe. As a result of this, we wasted around $350m^3$ over the course of a year. Quite apart from the expense, this was a mortifying blow for a family treating water as a precious commodity. Remember, too, to lag pipes and meter to prevent problems in the deep mid winter.

'How do I arrange for the telephone to be changed over?'

The telecommunications situation is complicated by an increasing number of private companies, all offering (apparently) something for nothing – until you read the small print. Although packages are now on offer that include the rental of the line itself, basically you pay your *abonnement* (rental charge) to France Telecom/Orange and then take your choice. You may, for example, choose to route your national and international calls via SFR, Bouygues Telecom or any number of smaller outfits offering deals to expats.

Your best starting point, therefore, is France Telecom/Orange (I think the company likes to be known now as Orange, while its detractors still use – with vitriol – the old name) . They will arrange for a new contract to be drawn up – and a new telephone number. This, incidentally, is always a ten-digit affair, usually quoted and memorised in pairs. The initial two numbers are cunningly grouped to indicate one of five geographic sectors of France, and the next two numbers denote the regional exchange. So our own '05' indicates the south-west, and the '65' indicates the Cahors exchange. Fiendishly clever, you must agree.

With such a plethora of companies and special offers, you may wish to try the Orange English-speaking helpline. It used to be free. Now the service is charged at the 'standard rate' and an American voice welcomes you to 'Awnge' (a sign of the times, as the artist formerly known as Prince might have observed). If you care to take the plunge, the number is (+33) (0)9 69 36 39 00.

'How do I ensure that the services don't get cut off during absences?'

None of these companies gives you much time to pay your bills. If you're planning to use the house only as a holiday home, I would strongly recommend you to set up a direct debit (*prélèvement*) for every service provider. You can arrange for the bills to be sent to your UK address, but by the time you receive one, there won't be much time left to send out the necessary payment. Having said that, I've always found that staff are generally (but not always!) reasonable if you explain any problems that you might have with payment and such like. If you're comfortable with technology, you can also usually arrange to pay your bills via the Internet.

'How do I go about insuring the house?'

I have mixed feelings about insurance in France. For a considerable time, I felt the service was cheaper and more efficient than it was in the UK. However, competition seems to be so fierce back home that you can shop around more extensively and probably find a better deal.

Les assurances, for a nation as paranoid as the French, are big business. So you will find plenty of choice in your nearest sizeable town: AXA, MAAF, MAIF and other big specialist companies, along with all the banks will offer you insurance for your house and its contents. Since their rates are all fairly competitive, you might be best starting off at your bank – since it's more in their interest to keep you 'sweet' and it's simpler for you to arrange payment of the annual premium.

We've already mentioned the *assurance dommages-ouvrage* that a vendor would take out when constructing a new property. You are legally obliged to carry this kind of third-party insurance (*civil propriétaire*) when you move into your accommodation or start work on the new house you are planning to build. You would also be advised to take out a comprehensive *assurance multirisque* to insure the house and its contents against most eventualities. When arranging this, take with you – if possible – some sort of plan of the house, because the advisor will base his or her assessment on the (approximate) habitable surface area of the property.

'How do I go about arranging medical insurance?'

It was only when Deborah slipped and broke her arm on Christmas morning 2005 that the reality of living here uninsured hit home. While she and our daughter were covered by the exorbitant national (and top-up) medical insurance that my wife pays every month, I blithely believed that I was still covered by the original E106 that I had to hand in at the Social Security office in Tulle not long after arriving here. In fact, I realised that a) I had lost the precious *Carte Vitale* they had sent me in response to my E106 and b) that it wasn't valid anyway because the E106 was not for life (as I had mistakenly believed), but for two years only.

So what should you do to ensure that you're not faced with a bill for some emergency hospital treatment? You should insure that you are at least covered in the short-term while you come out here to live or simply to get your property ready for letting purposes. The European Health

Insurance Card (EHIC) superseded the old E111, which is still imprinted on the national consciousness, but no longer accepted by the medical authorities here. With it, you are treated as a French citizen would be – which means that your bills would be reimbursed at around 70 per cent of the cost of the treatment. Most French citizens will take out a private *mutuelle* (top-up insurance) to cover the shortfall. Health care in France, though admittedly excellent, can cost a (sound) arm and a leg.

Within the UK, you can apply for an EHIC either online via the website www.ehic.org.uk or by phoning the Overseas Healthcare Team on 0191 218 1999. The card is valid for up to five years, but is not intended for stays abroad of more than six months. Effectively, therefore, you have a six-month cushion once you have chosen to live here permanently. After that time, the EHIC is invalid and you should return it to the section that issued it. However, there are a number of special arrangements that may apply according to your circumstances, so you should check the NHS or Department of Work & Pensions websites or phone the Overseas Healthcare Team for more details.

Generally, you have a number of options. If you are living and working here, you are obliged to join the *Sécu*, as the French *sécurité sociale* is known. If you are working for an employer, he or she will normally arrange this for you automatically. You then both pay regular contributions to cover you and your dependants for sickness, health care, unemployment and old age. If it's not done automatically, you will have to register personally at the local branch of CPAM (Caisse Primaire d'Assurance Maladie – or local health authority).

If you are self-employed, the procedure is more complicated. According to your profession, you will need to join the appropriate scheme. Most come under the umbrella of URSSAF (the Union de Recouvrement des Cotisations de Sécurité Sociale et d'Allocations Familiales). Staff at your nearest branch (which you will find in the departmental *préfecture* or *sous-préfecture*) will register your self-employment and make the necessary arrangements to ensure that blood is squeezed regularly from the stone.

If you or your partner is in receipt of a long-term incapacity benefit, or you have reached the official UK retirement age and you are in receipt of the state pension (and not in receipt of a pension from any other EU provider), you can apply for an S1. With this, you (and your partner in most circumstances) will be affiliated to the CPAM and therefore protected by long-term cover.

Otherwise, the only option left to you is the CMU. The Couverture Maladie Universelle entitles any resident of France who can show regular and 'stable' residence here for not less than 90 days in the year to apply for affiliation to CPAM. Whether this is free or subject to a contribution depends on your level of income.

Whichever of these applies to your own circumstances, you will – eventually – be issued with a social security number and a *Carte Vitale*, which looks like a green credit card and which indicates your entitlement to use state services and be reimbursed for a percentage of the cost. Don't – like I did – lose your card, because you will have to write to your regional CPAM and wait another eternity for a replacement. When you consult a doctor or pick up prescription drugs, you present your card and the information is logged on a central database. You must pay your *facture* for the visit or the prescription, but the information logged via the card ensures that you are reimbursed fairly swiftly. Rest assured, though, that you will not have to pay any exorbitant hospital bill before reimbursement. Her *Carte Vitale* covered my wife's treatment. Had it not, Christmas 2005 would have been truly wretched.

'How do I register with a local doctor?'

'Any time, any place, anywhere…' as the old Martini ad went. There was a time when every French citizen could go to as many doctors as they wanted any time, any place, anywhere. Being a nation of hypochondriacs, people did –

and still do. The slightest snuffle and off they go to the doctor for their appointment and their prescription for all the *cachets* necessary to ward off the Black Death. Understandably, the government has tried to regulate things – to protect the hard-pressed doctor and, most importantly, the state coffers. Citizens are now encouraged to choose one local doctor and stick to him or her. Before you do this, talk to people and get a feel for doctors' individual strengths and specialities. For example, because we are so suspicious as a family of pharmaceutical drugs, our local doctor specialises in homeopathy. When you have chosen someone you think might suit your needs, just go along to the *cabinet* (surgery) and register with the doctor (which you can do either before or when you have a specific medical need). You and the doctor should complete and sign form S3704 (a *déclaration de choix du médecin traitant*), which is issued by and returned to the local CPAM so your registration can be logged. If you find that the doctor isn't for you after all, then you have the right to try someone else.

Provided that your doctor is *conventionné* (officially recognised), your visits will carry a set fee (around €30), which is reimbursed at around 70 per cent. You will pay a little more for home visits, night calls and consultations on Sundays and public holidays. If you need an *ordonnance* (prescription), your doctor issues you with some illegible paper work, which you present at any pharmacy. You will be asked to pay for the medication, which is then reimbursed via the information scanned from your *Carte Vitale* at anything up to 100 per cent.

Q. 'How do I enrol my child(ren) at the local school(s)?'

Talking of insurance, when it's time for your child(ren) to go to the local school, they will also need a policy: an annually renewable *assurance scolaire*, which covers them in the event of any mishaps at school or on school trips. So if your daughter were to bury the hatchet in young Benjamin's head, for example, you as parents would be covered by her insurance. It may never come to that.

We enrolled our daughter for school at the appointed time (which is around March every year) a few months after her second birthday. This is a two-stage affair. The first stage was to enrol her at the local *mairie*. Since we weren't married in France, we couldn't produce the customary *livret de famille*, but had to show instead a *fiche d'état civile* (which the mayor's secretary issued and completed for us) in respect of our daughter. We also had to prove that we lived where we said with the usual utilities bill. Finally, and rather nervously, we had to show her *carnet de santé* (a kind of condensed medical file). This is supposed to show that your child has received all the necessary vaccinations. Since Deborah had treated her since birth with essential oils and studiously avoided any of the normal vaccinations, I was sure that this would be our High Noon. No school would ever take our little girl. In fact, the word 'CONTRAINDICATIONS' (meaning potential reaction in a patient with specific health problems, such as asthma) scrawled across the vaccination section seemed to satisfy them. I learned that this is one of the few advantages of being an *étranger*: if Tilley had been born in France, we would surely never have got away with it so lightly. Both of us would have been thrown into jail or burnt at the stake for apostasy, while our daughter would have been taken into care. But no, we were issued with the necessary *certificat d'inscription*.

With this, we could go about enrolling her at a school of our choice: the second stage of the process. Since she was now *propre* (out of nappies), we were able to start Tilley at the *école maternelle* in the adjacent commune right after the Easter holidays. Just a couple of mornings per week at first, to ease her into the straightjacket of a school pupil. She hasn't looked back.

Q. 'What do I need to do about my car and driving license?'

When we moved over here with a light green third-hand Golf on its last wheels, it was at a time when a standardised EU form of driving license was being introduced. We heard various differing information: we may or may not have to take another test over here before we could get our new license. By now I was a fully-fledged driver and the thought of having to learn how to overtake on brows of hills and blind bends, how to master the technique of tail-gaiting and how to unlearn my natural predisposition to stop for pedestrians when black and white stripes are painted on the road… well, it filled me with horror. Mercifully, it didn't come to that. We had to go down to the *préfecture* in Tulle with passports, photos, UK driving licenses and car papers. We exchanged our pink UK permits for pink French ones. Now, officially, you don't need to do this: your UK *permis de conduire* is valid here. Whichever version you hold, you must remember to take it with you whenever you get into your car. It is illegal to drive without one. These days, there are more intimidating *gendarmes* on the road than you can shake a baton at, and they are on the look-out for any excuse to issue a spot-fine – and augment the national treasury.

Nor would I recommend losing your license. Yes, of course, I managed to do just this. It necessitated a trip to the local *gendarmerie*, where two towering males with moustaches dealt with me (rather courteously, I should add) and issued a temporary paper. I then had to arrange and attend a medical, during which my eyes were tested along with my ability to walk in a straight line. Finally, I had to travel down to the *préfecture* in Cahors with a range of papers – excluding the one item that a draconian jobsworth on reception claimed barred me from the inner sanctum of public servants. Having already driven something like 80 kilometres, I didn't feel much inclined to take no from this charming creature. I barged past the barrier to said inner sanctum where I found a human being, who allowed me to sign something in lieu of my wife and who accepted my money and my documents with grace and understanding. I now have my replacement license and I keep it close to me at all times. It seems, though, that I am no longer qualified to tow a trailer.

One can import a car legally for up to six months without having to complete all the otherwise obligatory customs documentation. Any longer than this and you have to pay TVA on the car – either at the port or at your local tax office – in return for a certificate that allows you to register it in France. Then – within three months of entry – you contact the local DRIRE (Direction Régionale de l'Industrie et de la Recherche) to arrange an inspection of the car at a local inspection centre. If it meets all the necessary regulations, you will receive a DRIRE certificate that then allows you to apply for a certificate of registration at the *préfecture*. This is the famous *carte grise* and every car should have one. Losing one of these would be even more painful, and costly, than losing your license (and no, this is one document that I haven't – so far – managed to lose). At the *préfecture*, you will be given a daunting list of documents to furnish, which includes proof of ownership and all kinds of certificates. When, finally, we were handed our *carte grise*, we celebrated by driving to the far hills and eating vegetarian omelettes in the only restaurant open. It was one of the very best of too many omelettes we've eaten here.

You thought that was it...? Oh no. Within 48 hours of receiving your registration document, you must go to a garage and get your new plates made up and fitted. Surprisingly, this doesn't cost as much as you might fear. Altogether, though, it's an expensive and time-consuming business.

If it all sounds terribly complicated, be comforted by the fact that you can drive around in your car with a GB sticker for up to 90 days before there is any question of duty to pay. Some manage to get away with it for considerably longer than this. The gendarmes, however, might not be amused to find out just how long.

Q. *'What do I need to do about the local taxes?'*

To recap, we're talking here about the *taxe foncière* (on the property and land) and the *taxe d'habitation* (on its residents). If you're buying the property to let to tenants, you will be liable to pay the former, while the tenants will pay the latter. If you are an owner-occupier, you have to pay both. You will be exempt from the former for two years if your property is a new build or a rural conversion.

There is little for you to do other than to pay the bills (again, I would suggest that you arrange direct debit facilities unless you fancy doing it via the French government's fiscal website, www.impots.gouv.fr), because the *notaire* will inform the tax authorities of the change of ownership as part of the contractual process. You should note that whoever owns the property on the 1st January will be liable to pay *taxe foncière* for the whole year. However, *taxe d'habitation* is paid on a pro-rata basis. The *notaire* will arrange for you to refund your share to the vendor (who will have paid for the full year in advance).

Q. *'How do I go about applying for planning permission?'*

This will probably be one of your most pressing concerns. Having thought about, planned and priced all the work necessary to get your new property into shape, you'll want to get your application for planning permission in as soon as possible. In all but the most exceptional cases, you should have your basic C.U. To remind you: as a general rule of thumb, anything major (see below) requires a *permis de construire*; anything of fairly low importance (such as a swimming pool or a small extension) requires only a *déclaration des travaux*. Both require some kind of plans, but the procedure is less onerous for a simple declaration.

You will almost certainly need a *permis de construire* if your proposed work: significantly alters the appearance of the building (barn conversions, say, because you will need to put in doors and windows among other things); involves a change of use (again, changing an agricultural building into a

166

residential one; or changing a house into business premises); creates additional levels within the existing construction (adding a floor, for example).

You can get hold of the necessary application forms at the local *mairie*. Then you have to put together the dossier. This is no minor undertaking. When I presented our dossier last time, the (somewhat amateurish) drawings I'd done on Microsoft Word were eyed with ill-disguised contempt. You'll also need a photograph of the original building and some kind of edited photograph that shows what it will look like after the work has been carried out. You'll need maps and cross-sections and floor plans with measurements to scale. The entire planning-permission process was overhauled in 2007. As a result, all applications for a *permis de construire* now have to be submitted via a qualified architect **unless** you are an individual submitting an application for his or her own property if, on completion, the total habitable surface area is less than 170 square metres.

After dropping off the dossier at the *mairie*, you can expect to wait around three months for the result. Within a fortnight of submission, you will receive a letter with a registration number to quote in the event of a query, along with a date by which you should receive your decision. The letter suggests that if you haven't heard by this date, you can assume that approval has been granted. Again, recent experience suggests that this assumption can be rash. A fortnight after the date passed, I phoned the town hall to speak to the terse man who was 'following' our dossier – to discover that my customary fears were this time justified. There was indeed a problem (that we subsequently had to resolve).

'Can I start work on the house before I receive my permission?'

Technically speaking, you shouldn't start the work until you have received approval (which comes via the *mairie* from the DDE, Direction Départementale de l'Equipement, or more properly now the real DEAL, or Direction de l'Environnement, de l'Aménagement et du Logement). Some friends with a barn nearby sat around for months, waiting patiently and obediently to start work, getting cold and miserable in the process. Several phone calls did little to reassure them. On the very day they decided to jack it all in and go back to the UK, they received a favourable decision. By then, it was all too late. *Entre nous*, you could always start work on anything that's not going to be too noticeable from the outside and won't create any potential conflict with neighbours. A bit of low-key destruction is very therapeutic while you wait and fret. Obviously, though, don't start anything that realistically you may not be allowed to do or you might find that you have to undo it and pay a fine into the bargain.

'*What should I do when I get it?*'

Assuming that your *permis* is granted, you must declare your building site open at the *mairie* by completing a *déclaration d'ouverture de chantier*. As part of this, you must get hold of a big plastic notice from a builders' merchant, fill in the necessary details (which always get washed away by the rain, no matter how indelible the ink) and post it on prominent display. Simultaneously, a notice of the *permis* is placed in the local town hall and the dossier is available for inspection at the local DDE offices. If some wiseacre wants to object to what you are doing, he or she has two months in which to do so (and can actually insist that you stop the work). Moreover, if you fail to fulfil your part of the bargain, anyone has the right to object to your building work at any time within the next *30* years!

Q. '*Should I use an architect?*'

With hindsight – and unless this house falls down within the next few years – we were lucky to have found our eccentric architect (but then I like eccentrics and they always give value for money). I have heard some horror stories about architects, British and French. So-called professionals who have made elementary mistakes and fleeced their clients in the process.

We weren't legally obliged to use an architect because our new house's projected *SHON (Surface Hors Oeuvre Nette)* (a formula roughly equivalent to total habitable surface area, but involving a rather more complicated calculation) was less than 170 square metres. Nevertheless, because we were building in straw on a prominent site, we felt it would be politic to employ one at least for the initial stage of the process. We found it very reassuring to have our man with the beaded beard: an objective third party, someone to call up and consult at times of uncertainty or when your own particular view was diametrically opposed to that of an artisan. It was money well spent – but be careful whom you choose.

Their fees tend to be around 8–12 per cent of the estimated total cost of the construction or renovation, depending on the extent to which you are intending to use the architect's services. It will cost a lot less, for example (upward of €3,000) if you are using the architect to design the concept, produce some drawings and put together the dossier for the *permis de construire* than it would if you were using his or her services to produce a plan of works and a set of very detailed drawings, chase up estimates from artisans and oversee that the work is done *comme il faut* from start to successful finish. It will cost less on paper, but if you're not here all the time to oversee things yourself, or if you haven't a trusted friend or builder to do it for you, could it not end up costing more if things are just left to drift?

As a kind of halfway measure, you could also consider using a *maître d'oeuvre*. A 'master of works' who can (if trained in architecture) produce the detailed drawings, co-ordinate the collection of estimates and help you select the artisans to use, oversee the project and generally do most of what you might expect from an architect at rather less cost.

'How do I go about finding one?'

We started our search by going to a national advisory body (the CAUE, or Conseil d'Architecture, d'Urbanisme et d'Environnement) for an objective opinion about our plans and some assistance with finding a suitable architect. Gilles had actually worked at one stage for the CAUE and they knew of his reputation and interest in things a little 'alternative'. We went to see him and two others recommended by different friends.

After our interview in Gilles' alarmingly chaotic office, I really wasn't sure that I could work with someone who smoked so much and talked so fast. He seemed dangerously like a madman. Nevertheless, we went to look at some of the work he had shown us in his portfolio. We liked what we saw. Still not convinced, I telephoned a former client for his experience of working with a man who threads beads in his beard (not that I, as a former hippy, am against someone wearing beads in his beard, but it's just that our project, our life-savings, depended on the man). The former client's verdict was extremely positive. So when, at long last, we got to see his first computerised drawings and recognised that they bore, quite serendipitously, an uncanny resemblance to my wife's sketch (previously vetoed on budgetary grounds), we knew that he had to be our man. It was pre-ordained. And, thankfully, we never had cause to regret our choice.

So, how else might you find the right architect? You could talk to friends and/or estate agents. You could talk to builders (who generally have fairly outspoken views about architects and may recommend someone that they are happy to work with – although is this because the architect is good at his or her job, or because the architect is too laissez-faire and reluctant to challenge something that might be of concern? Worth considering). You could use the Pages Jaunes (the French Yellow Pages). Or you could try the website www.architectes.com, which (among other things, such as specimen contracts) can help you find architects for your particular region. You can also find a list of architects who specialise in environmentally friendly homes at www.cr3e.com.

'Should I carry out the project manager role myself?'

The alternative to getting an architect or a master of works to do all this for you is to undertake the role yourself. Having done this myself, I can vouch for the fact that it is very time-consuming, nerve-wracking and stressful. It's not really something you should contemplate doing on an intermittent basis – in other words, popping over from the UK from time to time to see how things are progressing. In all probability, they won't be. You need to be there or thereabouts all of the time if only because there will be questions – often crucial questions – that need quick (yet considered) answers. I installed myself in a caravan with a telephone right next to the site virtually every single day of the build, which lasted nearly a year. Without wishing to suggest that I have all of these qualities in spades (though I know I could do a much better job *next* time around), you'd need: a reasonable level of French, patience, energy, drive, determination, a certain amount of diplomacy, attention to detail, resilience, basic project management skills and a good sense of humour. I'm a thin man at the best of times, but over the course of that *annus horribilis*, I shed pounds with the worry and the physical work, and by the time we moved in, I resembled an escapee from the Siberian Gulag.

Q. 'How do I go about finding suitable artisans to carry out the work required?'

If you are prepared to go through all this yourself, then you – rather than your representative – will need to think about the best way to find the artisans you are going to work with in glorious harmony over many months. You have to make a fundamental choice: do you want to work with British workmen or French artisans (or both)? I opted for a combination of both, because my underlying criterion was that I wanted to work with people I liked as human beings.

And it just so happened that I knew a fair few Brits in the area and trusted them as personal friends.

Because of the language barrier, it's tempting to go for the apparently easier option and employ British workmen. It's so much easier to communicate: to make your wishes known and to understand their ideas and viewpoints. But consider the success story of an acquaintance of mine. He and his wife bought a house for renovation in Brittany. They made a conscious decision to use local artisans for every aspect of the project – and have been delighted with the results. They felt that these local workmen gave them real value for money and were prepared to go that extra mile for them. When I saw his photographs of the new roof and he told me what the local *couvreur* had charged him (€8,000), I was quite flabbergasted.

Local property developer, Tim Mannakee, concurs with this. 'I err much more to the French than the English. My most successful renovations have been with French artisans: particularly roofs, carpentry and stone masonry. As far as electrics, plumbing and plastering are concerned, it doesn't matter so much. The Brits will go by what they used to do in the UK, which may not be appropriate. And I find them expensive. They'll charge what they feel they can get away with, while the French tend to go by the prices in the book. So, be careful. Know a bit about their history.'

In order to find the right artisans, French or Brits will often advertise (albeit in different publications). We found our carpenter and now long-standing friend in the small ads of *France Magazine*. French artisans may advertise in the small ads of local papers or even on cards in supermarket foyers. However or whether they advertise (and there's an argument that suggests that the best don't need to advertise anyway), there's no substitute for word of mouth. Ask people. Ask your estate agent; ask your *notaire*. Ask your new neighbours. Drive around and you're bound to see building in progress. Talk to the proprietors; talk to the tradesmen. Talk to someone at the *mairie*; talk to someone at your local *boulangerie*. The building community is quite a small world. If you unearth someone you think you can work with, he'll certainly have plenty of colleagues in associated trades. And some now work in consortia, able to carry out almost every aspect of the job.

Having identified your potential workers, go and see some jobs they have been or are involved with and talk to their clients *before* you make your decision. You wouldn't buy a new car without test-driving it first. It sounds elementary, but I once engaged someone because I liked him so much and then placed myself in the unenviable position of having to 'disengage' him after seeing something that worried me.

'What do I need to know about hiring French workmen?'

Tim talked about French artisans often pricing work as per 'the book'. Deborah and I often laugh about the tendency of French people to live their whole lives according to the book, but this trades book is a different book to our fictitious one that's issued to every new French citizen at birth. It includes guideline prices for almost every conceivable type of work in the building trade and you can even get hold of it yourself (though it's expensive and the costs are based around new-builds, which often bear little resemblance to those for renovations).

By preference, you should employ *local* artisans. Not only will they be familiar with any quirks and traditions associated with the locality, but also their reputation counts on their doing a good job, and it's good PR for you as a newcomer to the area (provided, that is, that you pay people punctually and properly). As locals, too, you can check that they are registered at a local *mairie* and therefore have the obligatory '*SIRET*' number issued by the Chamber of Commerce and indicating registration for TVA. If they are not, then they may be working *au noir* (on the black) and that's ill-advised for a newly arrived foreigner hoping to be accepted by the community. Moreover, you will have no legal recourse if things go wrong. If the artisan is completely legal, there will be a whole raft of guarantees and mandatory insurances (remember that you must arrange the essential *assurance dommages-ouvrages* at the opening of the *chantier* or site) that will protect you over the course of the next few years in the event of damage or malfunctions.

The detail of the work to be carried out and, very often, a schedule of payment will be spelt out in a contract between you and your artisan. Don't pay any money up front before you have signed the contract. And don't sign the contract until you have checked its details carefully. If there's anything that worries you about it, ask for clarification. If you need an impartial view on it, you can consult the ADIL.

'How can I ensure that the work is carried out?'

The stereotypical French builder is, of course, someone who never turns up when promised to start the work – and someone who then leaves halfway through the work that he has eventually started.

There is, I have to say, an element of truth in this, but there are ways of ensuring that it doesn't happen to you. For a start, when you are choosing your artisan, don't just select someone on the basis of price or competence (or indeed personality). Get the individual to give you an *honest* appraisal of when he can start work. The French term *quinze jours* is the Gallic equivalent of *manana*. If someone tells you that he will start work in a fortnight, be sceptical. It's odds-on that he *won't* start work when promised. If, however, he tells you that because of his other commitments, he can't really hope to start for at least another three months, then this sounds much more plausible. It's then up to you to remind him of any promised start date. Be a little pushy; get on the phone and chase things up – firmly but politely. Both parties are going to benefit from good, clear, regular, even-tempered communications.

Bearing in mind that just about every artisan in France (unless they are really bad at what they do, in which case they won't be able to survive long in the system) seems to be

buried in work – much of it probably commissioned by immigrants like us – you should book them up as far in advance as it is practical to do so. The bigger the job, the bigger the delay will be, because they won't be able to squeeze you in between client x and client y. Line up your roofer even before you have signed for the house: good *couvreurs* are worth their weight in gold. Prioritise the work and, wherever possible, plan the sequence in which things will be done to tie in with your artisans' availability. Tim's experience is that French artisans will work 'very hard and efficiently – but you've got to keep on top of things; you can't let them drift. And pay people on time,' he adds. 'It's death to a site not to do this.'

Once things really get going, then a natural momentum builds up and your team will knuckle down to the task of finishing what they have started. If, by chance, work stops without any apparent good reason, you should contact the individual – by phone or by letter – and remind him of any agreement you have made about finish dates (*la réception*, as it's known). If appropriate, you can warn him that you will stop any payments scheduled until the work recommences. And if that doesn't work – and you don't have any influential Mafia connections – you can go to your local county court (*tribunal de grande instance*) and ask for a judicial ruling. But, of course, you wouldn't want to go this far unless you were desperate and quite sure of your grounds and had taken some kind of legal advice.

'What happens when the work is finished?'

Strictly speaking – if everything is being done by the book – your builder will inform you when all the work is finished. This date – *la réception* – is important for a number of reasons. It's the date from which all the various guarantees become effective. And it's your chance to inspect what has been done and make sure that it meets your satisfaction before you make any final payment. If you have been using an architect or a *maître d'oeuvre*, then he or she should accompany you – along with all the different professionals involved – on a thorough tour of inspection. If you are doing it all yourself, you have officially eight days within which to do this and raise any objections you might have.

Assuming that things have been done properly, you can make any final payments and officially close the *chantier* (site) by completing and sending or handing in at the *mairie* (within 30 days of the finish) a *déclaration d'achèvement des travaux*. You declare that the 'works have been achieved'. If the habitable surface area of the building has not yet been assessed, it won't be too long before someone official drops by with a tape measure to size you up for your *taxe d'habitation*.

At a later date, as we've discussed, any gas and electrical installations will need to be checked by the organisation that awards the certificates of conformity. Your new *fosse septique* will also be inspected to ensure conformity with the new regulations. Generally speaking, however, there is little follow-up of your original *permis de construire* in France. In the UK, the inspectors are always dropping by to check up on things. Only the tape-measurers, however, came by to scrutinise our new house.

'What redress do I have if it's not carried out to my satisfaction?'

As Tim Mannakee – who has been both customer and builder at different points – suggests, it shouldn't really come to this if you (as client and project manager) have communicated regularly and effectively with your artisans. If you haven't been around the site on a regular basis, you should remember that very often your builders will have had to make decisions – in good faith – on your behalf. Remember, too, that there may be apparent defects through no fault of the tradesman concerned: doors, for example, can be fitted with precision only to swell and stick in the weeks, even days, that follow; tiles may be bought in two batches with very slight variations in the manufacture, which can blemish a perfectly straight line. With old houses, too, it's virtually impossible to do things as perfectly as some customers might demand. It's often a matter of compromise and being reasonable.

My own experience so far is that people will usually put things right without making a '*pâté*' of the issue. Their professional pride and reputation are at stake, after all. Of course, if Professional X takes exception to Client-who-knows-diddly-squat Y questioning his competence, then you might have to get a little heavier handed. You can threaten to withhold part of the payment, for example (legally speaking, a final 5 per cent is held back until after all the work has been finished and you have carried out your inspection). If, however, the situation gets desperate, you can demand that any ongoing work is stopped and take the matter to court. It would have to be really desperate, though.

If you discover something untoward or unsatisfactory once the work has been carried out and your tradesmen have packed their toolboxes and left the site, then phone or visit the appropriate person before you start invoking any guarantees or threatening legal action. Appealing to their pride or better nature might just be sufficient.

Q. 'How can I ensure that the house is looked after during absences?'

It's always a worry to leave a property unoccupied for any length of time. What about squatters? What happens if there's an act of God? What happens if a ten-ton truck skids on the road and ends up as a feature in the fireplace? Any fellow neurotic will understand the kinds of worries that preoccupy one.

Obviously, you need to ensure that you are insured against all such eventualities. Then you need to find someone you can trust – one of your new neighbours perhaps – who will check the house on a regular basis and contact you in the event of anything that needs your attention. This might be easier said than done if the house is somewhere by the sea. Many of the houses nearby are likely to be holiday homes. Out in 'the sticks', we always found that there was no shortage of attentive neighbours willing to keep a spare key and look in from time to time.

If the idea of giving someone a key and therefore a tacit license to snoop worries you, well you can always pay someone to provide the service. You could ask your estate agent if he or she knows of anyone in the area, or you can check the small ads in the back of France Magazine or a similar publication. With the proliferation of *gîtes*, there has been a corresponding proliferation in small private enterprises to manage people's *gîtes* for absentee owners. Some such enterprise might be ideal for the job and happy to keep a watchful eye on your property for a modest fee.

'What should I do about the pool?'

Following the advent of fairly stringent new regulations, you should pay particular attention to arrangements concerning any swimming pool that comes with the property. Precipitated by a French politician's family tragedy (or so the hearsay goes), the ensuing regulations oblige pool-owners to take responsibility for their watery death-traps either by means of an alarm (fabricated in France and nowhere else), a surrounding fence (with lockable gate), or a sufficiently rigid pool cover. So before you go back to the UK and leave everything fallow for months at a time, make sure that you have carried out the necessary security measures – and give whomsoever is looking after the house any relevant instructions and/or keys. Remember, too, that winters can be severe and water in pumps and pipes can freeze, so also make sure that you have wintered the pool conscientiously. If in doubt, contact the installers and get them to give you some literature and/or to go through the procedure with you. Don't learn the hard way!

Q. *'How do I go about letting the house?'*

You may have bought your house specifically to rent out on a long-let basis or you may be comforted by the idea of having someone installed in the house when you're not there – and paying you a bit of money for the privilege. If the latter is the case, you shouldn't have any problems finding someone who is maybe renovating their own property and wants to spend the winter somewhere a little more comfortable than a building site.

The first thing to consider is that you won't get as much per week as you would for a holiday rental in high, medium or even low season. If you want to attract someone who's prepared to take over the house for, say, the three months of winter, you may have to compromise rather than hope to receive 12 times the weekly low-season rent that you have budgeted for in your business plan. In return, you can comfort yourself with the thought that your house will be occupied, heated and (hopefully) cared for.

Whether you're hoping to attract, let's say, a retired couple or a young family, you should consider your policy towards pets before someone puts you on the spot with an awkward question. You may also want to consider whether you are prepared to let people store their clobber in your barn or garage for the duration of the let (if it's not officially part of the rented accommodation). And you'll want to address the issue of heating: whether you charge an all-inclusive rent or require the tenants to pay for their heating on top of a basic rent.

Unless (or some cynics might care to substitute the phrase 'particularly if') they're close friends or members of your family, you will need to draw up some kind of legal document to specify rules and rights.

'*What are my rights as owner?*'

Since France is a republic founded fundamentally on socialist principles, the law does more to safeguard the rights of the tenant than those of the big bad landlord. In cases of unfurnished long-lets, for example, you sign an agreement with your tenant for a minimum of three years (for an individual) or six years (for a company). It's not possible to agree a shorter *bail* (tenure) unless you can give a valid reason according to the Residential Tenancy Act of 1989 or the property is furnished (in which case, it would last for at least a year). Moreover, the tenant is entitled to automatic renewal of the agreement at its expiry under the same terms. Landlords can only terminate the lease if they wish to reclaim the property for their own or their family's personal use; if they decide to sell the property (in which case, the tenant has first right of refusal); or if the tenant fails to pay the rent. Even if tenants fail to uphold their part of the agreement, eviction is far from automatic: it entails a complicated, exacting and drawn-out legal procedure. Even a judge's decision in your favour, as a friend has found out, doesn't necessarily represent the end of the saga.

The legal situation is less scary when it comes to seasonal lets. These are generally considered to be any period up to a maximum of six months. They are governed by the French *code civile* rather than the 1989 legislation. However, these provisions have to be supplemented by further requirements if the property falls under specific legislation such as Gîtes de France, or when the landlord is deemed to be a professional by dint of the number of properties in his or her portfolio. Both parties can agree the booking by phone or by Internet or via a brochure tear-off.

'What are the rights of a tenant?'

As you can see, tenants' rights are paramount. Even if they were to renege on their side of the agreement, you couldn't evict someone during winter. And you can't effectively sell the property or move into it with your family during the period of the bail. Not surprisingly, landlords are very cagey about letting their property under these terms.

With short-term lets, tenants have the right (unless stipulated in the agreement) of unrestricted use of the property and its facilities. And they can ask for damages or cancellation of the agreement if the landlord carries out work to the property that effectively renders (part of) it uninhabitable.

'What can I do to avoid any problems?'

You can do what most landlords do – and that is to be very circumspect about your potential tenants and spell things out as clearly and as unambiguously as possible in the tenancy agreement. Leave no grey areas to be exploited by a canny tenant.

With a short-term seasonal let, for example, you will need to send the tenant a detailed and accurate description of the property and its facilities. A failure to do this can be construed as misrepresentation on your part, which could trigger a cancellation of the lease or even a fine. The prospective tenant will confirm the basic agreement by sending a deposit. You have the right to use this as a penalty if the tenant then cancels the agreement – but you must stipulate this in writing.

Among the terms and conditions you will need to spell out in the lease agreement are: the length of stay and the amount of rent; the arrangements to cover the running costs of the house if these aren't included in the rent; policy on pets; any obligation on the tenant's part to take out civil liability insurance; and any restrictions on the use of the property. Once the lease is agreed between you, both parties are bound by its terms.

With a long-term let, you would be well advised to draw up a lease with the aid of an *agent immobilier* who offers this service, or – better still – your solicitor. A contract will set out names and addresses of the parties, provide a description of the property, and spell out the general conditions of the lease. You can also ask for a guarantor to be named, who will be responsible for payment of the rent in the event of the tenants' failure to do so.

The onus is on you – or your agent – to be diligent in checking the bona fides of your potential tenants. You can ask for proof of identity, proof of their current address and proof of their employed status as well as their ability to pay the rent you are asking.

Once you and/or your agent are happy about the choice of tenant(s), you can arrange for the contract to be signed. At this point, you should ask for a deposit of two or three times the monthly rent and keep this as some kind of guarantee against damages. You should return it to the tenants at the end of the contract. Wait until they have actually vacated the premises, because you will need to check the property thoroughly for any damage that might not have been immediately apparent. To help you make a methodical check, you should carry out a written inventory of the property's condition once you have agreed the terms, but before the tenants move in. You (or your agent) and the tenant should both sign this *état de lieux* (state of the place), as it's rather endearingly known.

'What is the role of an agent in the letting process?'

For roughly one month's rental income (half of which is paid by the tenants), an agent will draw up a contract and find your tenants. For a further month's rental, an agent will also manage the rental – by collecting the rent, overseeing the property and arranging for any repairs or general maintenance required. You will be advised to take out an insurance policy (costing roughly another 2.5 per cent of your rental income) that guarantees your rent in the event of the tenants reneging on their agreement. The agent's fee will also include his or her intervention in the event of any problems with payment and general behaviour of your tenants.

'What happens if I decide to sell the house?'

As we've already seen, you can't decide to sell up while you've got someone living in your house under a legal tenancy agreement. You need to wait until the contract has run its course. Then, in the case of long-term unfurnished lets, you must offer your tenant(s) first option to buy.

Q. 'How do I go about selling my house?'

This is, of course, a book about buying a house in France. However, maybe you've bought the house as an investment and, after three or four years, you find that its value has appreciated nicely, so why not take the profits? Or maybe, like us, you find that it's worked out well and you want to stay in France, but perhaps you're ready to try somewhere else.

So what are the options? You could perhaps, if you're in no particular hurry, do very little: just put the word out that you are hoping to sell the house and wait for someone to call at the door. It happens. What's more, you can afford to add a little to the asking price to take account of the fact that the purchaser won't be paying any agency fees. Or you could, as we did, post the details of the house on a website specialising in French houses for British property hunters. We didn't have to wait long, which suggests that we probably undervalued the house.

And that's the danger of not using an estate agent. They know the market better than you; they know what kind of property sells easily and for roughly how much. Indeed, the prevalent criticism of estate agents is that they have unnaturally inflated the market by persuading vendors to ask over the odds. One important thing to know about if you decide to sell your house via an estate agent is the different kinds of *mandats* (agreements) that exist. If you know and trust and love one agent in particular, you could sign a *mandat exclusif*, which means that he or she will be acting as your sole agent. On the other hand, you can sign a *mandat simple*, which means that this agent is only one of several representing you. If you do this, though, remember what it was like to be a property hunter. How frustrating it was to receive details of a likely property from your agent, only to find that it has been sold via another *agence immobilier*. So remember to keep a note of the different agents that have your *mandats*, and to keep them informed of any developments. Whichever option you choose, the agent cannot start showing prospective buyers around until you have signed that *mandat*.

When you have found your buyer, it's then a matter of going through the whole contractual process with a *notaire*, but this time from the vendor's point of view. And, as a vendor, it will be up to you to arrange for all those expensive surveys: energy, lead, asbestos, termites and who knows what by the time you come to sell your house.

'What are the fiscal implications of selling the house?'

Selling up could raise the spectre of capital gains tax. *Impôt sur les plus values*, to give it its proper title, is every bit as complicated as its UK equivalent. Essentially, it's a tax on the capital gain or difference between the original purchase price and the new selling price. The tax is levied at a rate of 34.5 per cent on the capital gain (capital gains tax at 19% plus the contentious 'social charges' at 15.5 per cent), but you can offset against the capital gain any legal and agents' fees relating to the sale, along with most registered artisans' bills relating to restoration, renovation or general improvement (as opposed to repair and maintenance) of the property – which is another good reason for not using artisans who work 'on the black'. Of course, this effectively penalises individuals who renovate a property themselves.

The taxable gain is reduced according to the length of time that you own the property. After 22 years, it reaches zero (though not for the social charges, which are zeroed only after a miserly 30 years). Stealth taxes being stealthy, a surcharge applies (from 2014) on capital gains of more than €50,000.

Anyway, let's try to remain philosophical and look at a few scenarios as a means of picking our way through some of the legal complexities.

If you are resident in France, with no real estate in the UK, and you decide to sell your house here, you will be treated as any other French resident. That's to say, capital gains tax is not paid on the sale of your principal residence or on profit from the sale of the first residential property bought to let to tenants. Anyone selling a second home who does not own his or her principal residence (in other words, it's rented or leased instead) is also exempt.

If you are considered non-resident (because you don't live and submit annual tax returns in France) and you sell your house here, it is treated as a second home and you will normally be subject to capital gains plus social charges (subject to the outcome of the EC's legal proceedings against France over the latter element). This is offset against any potential UK liability under the double-taxation agreement. Moreover, if the house sells (currently) for more than €150,000, the *notaire* handling the sale will employ an *agent fiscal accredité* (a kind of auditor) to carry out on your behalf an independent fiscal audit in order to determine your liability. A standard fee of 1 per cent of the selling price + TVA at 20 per cent, to be offset against the eventual capital gains liability, is payable.

Friends from London who sold their holiday home in a nearby village complained that this 'auditor' would not communicate directly with them, but only via the *notaire*. And since the *notaire* effectively represents the state, they had no one to represent their own interests. Although their estate agent's and *notaire's* fees, artisans' bills and original purchase price could all be offset against their capital gain, they discovered that artisans' receipts alone are not valid. You also have to prove actual payment by means of, for instance, bank statements – which means that theoretically you will need to keep bank statements for the full 15 years of potential liability to capital gains tax (which runs counter to current financial advice to keep as little information as possible on paper in view of the exponential growth in identity theft). Of the €185,000 that their house fetched, they paid around €10,000 in capital gains tax. Significantly, the fiscal agent picked on the (fully registered) English artisans they used for a complete audit trail. If it all sounds more than a little xenophobic, discriminatory and constitutionally unsound, the European Court came to the same conclusion in

2011. For the moment, however, fiscal agents are still used. After all, when has the EC actually managed to stop France doing precisely what it wants to do?

Although (since 1998) private individuals don't have to pay back TVA when selling their house, if you deal in property professionally or you bought the house as a SCI, you may have to. However, you either pay capital gains tax or TVA, not both. So if your property qualifies as a new build (which includes complete barn renovations) and your SCI sells it within five years of signing the *déclaration d'achèvement* (to say it's finished), you may have to pay TVA (at 20 per cent) – as opposed to capital gains tax – on your selling price. Again, you can offset TVA already paid to builders and for building materials.

SUMMARY

Regardless of your ultimate plans for it, now that you are the owner of the house, there are things to sort out in the short, medium and longer term. You can ask yourself, your agent, a friend and/or a neighbour some or all of the following questions:

✔ **What immediate steps should I take?**
   (Qu'est-ce qu'il faut faire immédiatement?)
   – What checks should I carry out at the property?
     (Quelles vérifications est-ce que je dois faire après l'achat?)
   – How do I arrange for the electricity/gas/oil/water/telephone to be changed over?
     (Comment je peux organiser le changement du contrat de l'électricité/gaz/mazout/l'eau/téléphone?)
   – How do I ensure that the services don't get cut off during absences?
     (Qu'est-ce qu'il faut faire pour être sûr que ces services ne soient pas coupés pendant mes absences?)
   – How do I go about insuring the house?
     (Comment je peux assurer la maison?)
   – How do I go about arranging medical insurance?
     (Comment je peux organiser l'assurance maladie?)
   – How do I register with a local doctor?
     (Comment est-ce que je peux m'inscrire auprès d'un médecin?)
✔ **How do I enrol my child(ren) at the local school(s)?**
   (Qu'est-ce qu'il faut faire pour inscrire mon/mes enfant(s) à l'école primaire / au collège/lycée?)
✔ **What do I need to do about my car and driving license?**
   (Qu'est-ce qu'il faut faire concernant ma voiture et mon permis de conduire?)

✔ **What do I need to do about the local taxes?**
(Qu'est-ce qu'il faut faire concernant les taxes locales?)

✔ **How do I go about applying for planning permission?**
(Comment je peux faire une demande de permis de construire?)

- Can I start work on the house before I receive my permission?
  (Est-ce que je peux commencer des travaux avant le permis?)
- What should I do when I get it?
  (Qu'est-ce qu'il faut faire quand je reçois le permis?)

✔ **Should I use an architect?**
(Est-ce qu'il faut employer un architecte?)

- How do I go about finding one?
  (Comment je peux en trouver un?)
- Should I carry out the project manager role myself?
  (Est-ce que je dois être le maître d'œuvres moi-même?)

✔ **How do I go about finding artisans to carry out the work required?**
(Comment je peux trouver des artisans pour faire des travaux?)

- What should I know about hiring French workmen?
  (Qu'est-ce qu'il faut savoir pour engager des artisans?)
- How can I ensure that the work is carried out?
  (Comment je peux être sûr que les travaux sont faits?)
- What happens when the work is finished?
  (Qu'est-ce qui se passe quand les travaux sont finis?)
- What redress do I have if it's not carried out to my satisfaction?
  (Quels sont mes recours si les travaux ne sont pas faits correctement?)

✔ **How can I ensure that the house is looked after during absences?**
(Comment je peux m'assurer que la maison est surveillée pendant mes absences?)

188

– What should I do about the pool?
(Qu'est-ce qu'il faut faire concernant la piscine?)

✔ **How do I go about letting the house?**
(Comment je peux louer la maison?)

– What are my rights as owner?
(Quels sont mes droits en tant que propriétaire?)

– What are the rights of a tenant?
(Quels sont les droits d'un locataire?)

– What can I do to avoid any problems?
(Qu'est-ce que je peux faire pour éviter des problèmes?)

– What is the role of an agent in the letting process?
(Quel est le rôle d'un agent dans la location d'une maison?)

– What happens if I decide to sell the house?
(Qu'est-ce qui se passe si je décide de vendre la maison?)

✔ **How do I go about selling my house?**
(Comment je peux vendre la maison?)

– What are the fiscal implications of selling the house?
(Quelles sont les implications fiscales si je vends la maison?)

'And in conclusion...'

Voilà, as they say. (There you have it.)

Admittedly, certain aspects (such as inheritance tax) can seem complicated and confusing, but generally it isn't very difficult to buy property in France. Sometimes it's more difficult to find the time necessary to clarify your own thoughts and ensure that you are motivated by the appropriate reasons. Where things go wrong, it's usually because a buyer hasn't really thought things through. Otherwise, it's a matter of being well prepared and patient enough to trust that even though the administrative wheels appear to turn slowly, they turn relentlessly. It *will* happen.

Whether you choose to live in it or not, being the owner of a house here gives you a profound insight into this endlessly fascinating country and its curious inhabitants. They can be charming, rude, endearing and utterly exasperating. Ultimately, I suppose, the success of your venture depends to some degree on how able you are to cope with such paradoxical people. After all these years here, our honeymoon period may be over and there may have been times when we've been perilously close to packing up, unable to cope for one minute longer with some of the more irksome quirks of life in France, but we're still hanging on in here – generally very happy and not at all ready to trade places with someone back in the UK.

Perhaps it's appropriate to end by referring one last time to the experience of others. It might – or might not – help you make your own mind up. I was chatting to someone who owns a holiday apartment in the area. He and his wife manage to get over four or five times a year, even if only for long weekends. These visits are so important because they give them glimpses of a way of life that seems to have been lost forever in the UK. Nevertheless, they couldn't imagine living here. They would miss everything that was familiar and reassuring about their part of England: family, friends and little regular rituals like trips to the local cinema with their youngest child on wet Saturday afternoons.

Then, sometime later, I was indulging with a good friend in a favourite pastime of ex-pats the world over: comparing life in the adopted country to life in the mother nation. My friend's parents-in-law have recently moved back to somewhere on the Lancashire coast. Although they enjoyed their ten or so years here, they find it exhilarating and liberating to be back in the UK. His daughter, on the other hand, spent virtually her entire childhood in France. She started at university in Manchester and found it exciting to be in England because it was so different to what she had known. However, she was totally bewildered and disenchanted by the prevalent youth culture – of going out to pubs and clubs and drinking as much as is humanly impossible. Interestingly, she then went to Italy to see her brother and fell in love with the place and the lifestyle. She's now moved out there and is as happy as could be.

Italy. Now there's a thought!

Other titles by Mark Sampson

It's July 2003. A tropical heat wave is raging and old people are dropping like flies in Paris. The Sampsons move from their happy home into a caravan that thinks it's a sauna. In 12 months they must build a house of straw on terrain as rocky as their practical credentials...

To anyone who struggles to pitch a tent, the prospect of building a grand design of straw bales – in *France Profonde* – could be somewhat unsettling. Some will tell you that building their own home is an enjoyable and rewarding experience; Mark Sampson will tell you it was hellish. Based on his journal of building the house seen on frequent re-runs of Channel 4's *Grand Designs*, this is a darkly comic account of a year of living uncomfortably close to the edge.

Less about the technical aspects of construction, *Bloody Murder* is more about the de-construction of family life in the face of a looming deadline, a shrinking budget, capricious conditions and a motley cast of tradesmen. Laugh, cry and wonder why.

The Thousands of people who watched charming Mark Sampson build his straw house on "Grand Designs Abroad" will be delighted to read this delightful and insightful book. On the TV programme Mark comes across as a reluctant builder and all-round amateur but as an author Mark is a real professional. Beautifully written, poignant, funny and heart warming Mark takes us behind the scenes of the human story behind the house build. We meet the real builders, TV crew, Kevin and Mark's family and Mark's inner demons. It's a great story. I recommend it to anyone.

Nigel Harrison

Find out more on Mark Sampson's Amazon author page: http://www.amazon.co.uk/Mark-Sampson/e/B008TRNU4Y?oo=41439047

About the Author

Mark Sampson is a writer, journalist and *book-maker* based in South-west France. Born in London and raised in Belfast, he studied English Literature at Exeter University and American Studies at the University of Sussex near Brighton, where he met his wife, Deborah.

They moved from Sheffield to France in 1995, not long after the birth of their daughter. They moved from the Corrèze to the Lot in 2003 to build the straw-bale house featured in the only series to date of *Grand Designs Abroad*.

Mark has written stage plays, screenplays, children's books and three books of non-fiction. The second, *Essential Questions to Ask When Buying a House in France* was updated in 2012 as his first eBook for Amazon Kindle.

As a journalist, he has written for most UK newspapers and many magazines, including *France Magazine* and *Living France*. As an on-line DJ for www.expatsradio.com, he also reviews Latin jazz and other world music for *Songlines*.

*****

connect with Mark Sampson

Facebook: https://www.facebook.com/mark.sampson.52035

Printed in Great Britain
by Amazon